Cuernavaca Sermons:

The Homiletical Accompaniment

to a

Congregational Reorientation

October 2015 – August 2016

Bruce W. Coggin

Copyright © 2017 Bruce W. Coggin

All rights reserved.

ISBN: 1548121231
ISBN-13: 978-1548121235

DEDICATION

This book is dedicated to the good people of St. Michael and All Angels Anglican Church in Cuernavaca, Morelos, Mexico.

Onward and upward!

CONTENTS

25 October 2015...12

01 November 2015...17

08 November 2015...21

15 November 2015...25

22 November 2015...29

06 December 2015...34

13 December 2015...39

24 December 2015...43

27 December 2015...45

03 January 2016..48

10 January 2016..52

12 June 2016...58

19 June 2016...62

26 June 2016...68

03 July 2016..72

10 July 2016..76

17 July 2016..80

24 July 2016..84

31 July 2016..88

07 August 2016...93

14 August 2016...97

ACKNOWLEDGMENTS

I am indebted to Tracie Middleton, deacon of the Episcopal Diocese of Fort Worth for help managing the arcana of formatting of this book. All word processors have the upper hand of me. She can make them sit up and beg.

I am indebted to Carrie Coggin Stanley, my younger daughter, for the photographs that illustrate this book.

I am indebted to Stephen Spencer, long the senior warden at St. Michael's, for sending for me when the parish found itself on a rocky road.

I am indebted to Sandy Acker, senior warden when these sermons were preached, and her husband Ed. Their support and hospitality shown to me and my family helped make it all a joy.

The entry of St. Michael and All Angels' Church. The supported A-frame building features rusticated stone and cement, elegant and austere, typical of mid-twentieth century Mexican architecture.

Introduction

If you've never been to Cuernavaca, I hope you get a chance to go one day, because it is one of the world's truly unique places, no place else like it. After Hernán Cortéz got through demolishing Tenochtitlan, he must have wondered where he'd set up shop and govern since the damage he did was extensive. I can imagine some native guide giving him the hint: "*Jefe*, you've pretty well ruined the old city, but let me tell ya, if you'll just ride on south a little, up and over the mountains, there's a place down there you just won't believe!" Sure enough, he came, he saw, and he stayed in some of the most delightful geography on the planet, swathed in what German explorer and naturalist Alexander von Humboldt swore was the world's best climate, an "eternal spring" in which the temperature is rarely below fifty, rarely above eighty Fahrenheit. The volcanic soil, the altitude, the abundant rain, and the year-round growing season produce vegetation whose variety and beauty are simply spectacular. The city has since the sixteenth century become one of the world's premier retirement destinations, the end of the Golden Road for a fairly heady company, including Cortéz, Emperor Maximilian, Betty Hutton, and the Shah of Iran. Thousands less notorious have also come there after long acquaintance with success, drawn by the ambience and the availability of amiable people willing to earn a modest living making life easy for a colorful, educated, often pampered ex-patriate community.

The place was not large until quite recently. In 1950, the population was around twelve thousand, and many of the present city's neighborhoods were then in fact outlying villages. In 1947, Malcolm Lowry's novel *Under the Volcano* brought Cuernavaca into a not altogether flattering kind of light. First written in a home—since converted into an eponymously styled hotel, Bajo el Volcán—situated at the upper end of Avenida Humboldt while the author, drunk a lot of the time, struggled with the break-up of his marriage, the book tells a lurid tale of the last day in the life of a British consul in an outpost called Quauhnahuac, an approximation of the Nahua name for Cuernavaca. A movie followed the book fairly soon, and Cuernavaca acquired a degree of notoriety as a place where mysterious things of a fierce and wonderful kind happen. Likely the proximity of Tepoztlán, one of Mexico's *pueblos mágicos*, contributed to the aura. At any rate, the place grew exponentially from the early 1960s and now has around a million inhabitants in the metropolitan area.

Far earlier, during the decades of Porfirio Díaz' reign as president (1876-1911) a good many English and Americans came to Mexico, lured by the advantages he offered foreign investors, and some of them ended up in Cuernavaca, not only to retire but also in commerce that ran from mining to dairying to agriculture to railroading and more. Near the end of the nineteenth century there were enough Anglicans from the British Empire and the United States to start a congregation, parented by Christ Church, Mexico City, a parish canonically connected to the U.S. Episcopal Church at the time. They dedicated the new congregation to St. Michael and All Angels and soon built a chapel at the corner of Guerrero and Degollado, scant blocks from the center of the city, large enough to accommodate about a hundred people. You can read all about it in the stain glass windows behind the altar in the building that today touts itself as "the world's smallest cathedral" and is the seat of the present Bishop of Cuernavaca of the Iglesia Anglicana Mexicana. The congregation worshipped and worked there into the 1960s when, for a number of reasons, they moved some miles northeast of the center of the city into a fashionable new neighborhood called Las Delicias and occupied a recently built chapel raised originally for a Spanish speaking congregation, San Pablo, which could not support the building. A simple concrete A-frame, the chapel adjoined a parish hall and another building housing the only English language library in the city.

I first found St. Michael's when I was invited to supply for about six weeks in the summer of 2006. The parish was temporarily without a rector, had been for some time, and depended on visiting clergy to provide liturgical and pastoral service. My friend the Rev'd. Gayland Pool was rector there some years back, and they asked him to come for a while; but he was busy that year. I had moved to Fort Worth the year before, had no steady church job, and he asked me if I'd like to go. You bet! I spent a lovely time getting to know the congregation—by then fairly small and fairly long in the tooth—and learning more about the city I first visited in the 1980s. I usually found anywhere from ten to twenty people in church Sunday mornings, everything in order and kept that way under the able leadership of Steve Spencer, Senior Warden for many years. I came again the next summer, and like the year before there was not a lot of work. Not long after, however, the congregation elected a new rector, the Rev'd. Tamara Newell, an American raised in Mexico, perfectly bilingual, perfectly bicultural, and perfectly smart. Believe you me, she transformed the place. I went back in the summer of 2009, found the church full on Sunday mornings, a talented choir mistress and choir singing to the accompaniment of a splendid new organ—and I do mean splendid—children under foot and children in expectant mommies' tummies, people involved in ministry to children outside the parish and among the elderly and the indigent (of whom Cuernavaca has the world's supply), the whole place really alive and making a wonderful racket! Since the city has no other English speaking congregation, Tamara welcomed many from other Christian traditions—some told me privily they were pretty agnostic but loved the community and ministry—and put everybody to work doing for others. Just breathtaking. You can bet I stayed plenty busy that summer, though after that year I was not needed again for some time.

In September 2015, however, I got an e-mail from Steve Spencer, moved from Cuernavaca to Ensenada for family reasons but still connected to the parish. His e-mail began: "Problems in Cuernavaca. Can you come for six months?" At this point in my life, I don't commit to *anything* for six months, but I said I'd do three, 15 October 2015 to 15 January 2016. Steve put me in touch with Sandy Acker, the Senior Warden, and she brought me up to date. Oh my. Circumstance had not been kind to St. Michael's. When Tamara reached retirement age, she retired, setting up a hard-act-to-follow situation. Along about the same time the grim reaper came through town and carried away some stalwarts. The mining industry in the State of Morelos collapsed, and a lot of young Canadians with children moved away, leaving a big hole. Mexico's political instability under President Calderón scared others off, none coming to replace them thanks to the vile anti-Mexico propaganda mill in the United States. If that weren't enough, the vestry elected a new rector just not equal to the task and burdened with serious personal problems that proved toxic to both him and the congregation. Evidently the place was in just about as bad condition as it could be in and survive, rather as if the doctor had to be summoned to the house because the patient likely wouldn't make it to the emergency room. In other words, right down my alley. I've spent a lot of my career in and out of church cleaning up other people's messes and re-directing the work, and I figured my task was to de-tox the patient, do CPR, get it into re-hab, and get it ready to elect its next rector. Boy, was I wrong.

I won't give you a play-by-play, but within a month I learned the congregation was in worse shape than I imagined and that my hardest job was not resuscitation but rather reorientation. I let people vent, contacted many disaffected, made physical plant improvements, re-established pastoral contact with the few sick and dying, all that with wondrous cooperation from the small handful of saints who kept the machine ticking over; but my efforts to stir up interest in this or that fell on ears more worn out than deaf. Not only had the critical mass decreased—forty in church was a big crowd—but also those who were there were a little . . . oh . . . gun shy about getting all ginned up again for the kind of parochial life they'd known just a couple years before. It came home to me that an ambitious priest might go nuts with frustration, and if the congregation was to select effective leadership going forward, a realignment of expectations and circumstances was unavoidable.

One thing's for sure: the people on whose shoulders the care of St. Michael's had come to rest were willing to listen, still hopeful, absolutely determined not to give up. God bless them, because I've seen people throw in the towel in the face of far less. I spent lots of time just jawboning with them and pondering and praying and thinking it over again and casting the net on the other side until we finally came up with a kind of consensus. St. Michael's had been, as my Grandmother Yeager used to say, jerked through a knot-hole and had a deal of healing to do, healing which would take time. Beyond that, circumstances beyond anybody's control made undertaking any vigorous new initiatives pretty hazardous, laden with potential for further frustration and disaffection. So we decided to ask the congregation to think of itself as a chaplaincy, a kind of chapel of ease, until circumstances and the Holy Spirit presented new avenues for ministry, even new growth—though I am not one who thinks churches have to be growing all the time, often think a little shrinkage is good for the whole outfit. Such a congregation did not need, could not use really, a priest full time, though it certainly needed a chaplain, someone to keep the prayer life alive and do pastoral ministry as needed. That chaplain also needed to understand that the congregation was in recovery and should not be stressed. Finally we decided the vestry should ask clergy to come for no less than a month (because travel and housing and a minimal stipend meant investment) and no more than three (because in that period no one could really ball things up too badly nor could much personality cult develop). The congregation would adopt its re-thought ministry: keep the doors open, keep the lights on, keep the prayers going, keep pastoral care available, keep its arms wide open to whatever walks in, wait and pray for the Lord to send a new day. And that's where I left things when I came home in January.

Of course, such a posture could be called poltroonery, I guess, but I think it was nothing more nor less than acquiescence to reality. Kipling is so good on what he calls India's two principal gods, the God of Things As They Should Be and the God of Things As They Are. One yearns for the former, but the latter gets you past the mileposts. Oh, they could have found some rip snortin' young priest somewhere who'd come down and chase himself or herself around town trying this and that or the next thing, but it would be largely a solo and would dissolve upon rip snorter's departure. The facts said: bed rest. Tamara and Gillian Ball, a priest retired of the Canadian Anglican Church, split the work for the late winter and spring, and I returned in June 2016 for a check-up. I have to say, the patient was responding really quite well. In the ten weeks I was there, I spent no time hearing horror stories, none arbitrating disputes, none agonizing, none managing stress. Sundays found from thirty to forty people at prayers, very little complaining about anything, a very relaxed, non-anxious atmosphere all round. Part of that came from a sage decision of the bishop, Enrique Treviño (offices and residence next door to the parish), who named Tamara Priest-in-Charge, even though she continues retired. It was a canonical nicety—no Mexican congregation can be without a priest-in-charge of some kind—but it sent a number of good messages through the ecclesiastical body. The people connect her with Good Times and Good Decisions; she's 100% One Of Us; she won't let anybody harm us; and even if she's not always nearby, she's always in touch. Brilliant move, I think. The result for me was something like a paid vacation with Sunday duties. All three of my grown kids came to visit—and said, "Now we know why you come down here." I gave the congregation the best I had on Sundays, visited with them socially the rest of the time, found myself at times wondering how to pass the time. The patient was definitely doing better and in a far, far better mood. And by golly, I had the joy of leading the first baptism in three years, not of a child but of an adult who came to us all by himself, found us meet, right and so to do, and asked for baptism. Hallelujah! By the time I came home, I felt pretty good about the whole experience, because I knew St. Michael's will, first, survive and, second, in God's good time thrive anew. I hope. I pray.

I am so grateful to all the various people who channeled me toward St. Michael's and those there who worked with me. I am not going to list names, first because I would surely omit somebody and, second, some of them would skin me for calling attention to them. But I promise you there are about a dozen, fifteen really dedicated workers there, people with real Jesus religion, with whom I would not be afraid to jump Hell with two buckets of water. I also should say that St. Michael's has a super-duper reputation in the city, because many wonderful people not members of the congregation hosted me and advised me and worked with me, and all together we made some tiny steps together on the road to reconciling the world to God through Christ Jesus Our Lord. My cup runneth over.

Bruce W. Coggin, Priest
Fort Worth, May 2017

The nave of St. Michael's Church. The nave accommodates around a hundred people comfortably in pews arranged with a center aisle and aisles on either side. The pews of Mexican hardwood display the traditional angularity of indigenous design. The floors are gray slate, the walls painted plaster over stone. The altar, wall cross, credenza, lecterns, aumbry, baptismal font, and other appointments are of lattice-work black wrought iron. Stain glass windows run from the entry to the sanctuary at head height. The choir sings from a loft above the entry, accompanied by a superb electronic organ. The building's hard surfaces produce very "sound fast" acoustics. The wall behind the altar, undecorated except for the cross, cries out for a talented muralist in the great national tradition to bring it alive with the triumphant archangel and his legions. Just sayin'.

25 October 2015

Twenty-second Sunday after Pentecost

Jeremiah 31:7-9 Psalm 126 Hebrews 7:23-28 Mark 10:46-52

Most of you said Amen a few minutes ago to the collect for the day, and if you didn't, we're going to play like you did. Do you remember it? It's a blockbuster. We asked God to increase in us the gifts of faith, hope, and charity; and we asked God to make us love what he commands so we might obtain what he promises. Remember? You said Amen to a mouthful, you and everyone in every Anglican or Episcopal church around the world, all the Roman parishes, all the Lutheran churches, lots of Methodists and Presbyterians, all Christians who worship according to the ancient traditions we never abandoned and so many more have come to share—a great lifting up of the soul of humanity to God in the anticipation that God will hear and act upon us.

Our petition to God comes in two parts, and the second part logically precedes the first. The language says God promises us something and commands us to behave so we may obtain that promise, which implies that we cannot obtain that promise without loving those commandments. The first part names a trio of virtues which evidently can help us learn to love those commandments and therefore obtain the promise, which in turn implies we need help. It's a complex prayer, but I think that is the internal logic.

I think that as Christians we know quite well what that promise is, namely life in what Jesus and the Bible call the Kingdom of God, of which more anon; and I think we know just as well what God commands. It's not new to us. It's the first commandment Moses came down the hill with, that we love God with all our heart, mind, soul and strength, to which God's son our Lord Jesus added the energizing gloss that we love our neighbors as we love ourselves, expanding the whole action of love from a dyadic to a triadic event: God loves us, and in amazed gratitude we love our neighbor so God's love may return whence it came as the neighbor learns of God's love from us. I have never quite figured out why, when all the liturgical reforms came down three decades or so ago, they decided to eliminate the repetition of those two commandments every time we gather at the table. And anybody who has the temerity to quibble, "And who is my neighbor?" need only check out the parable of the Good Samaritan.

Okay, I think we've got a grip on that. So how are we doing? Always loving the commandments and keeping them? Don't know about you, but I have to admit I don't get there all the time; and if you're anything like me, and I suspect you are, you probably don't get there all the time either. Oh, some of the time, yes, and thank God for that. I sometimes find myself doing things that amaze me, because being loving and giving is all too often not my default nature; and I remember on a previous visit here, this congregation was working alive with this or that project to share its bounty and its time and its love with the needy world that surrounds us here on all sides, and that's not quite so evident today. More often than not I fall short of the mark, and I won't ask for a show of hands from you. Evidently we need help.

Enter faith, hope, and charity. I figure you may recognize that trio at once as the culmination of a long passage in Paul's first letter to that troublous parish at Corinth that gave him such a fit . . . although in a half century of parish priesthood I remain impressed by how sedulously folks manage to avoid actual eye contact with a Bible. Do you know where yours is? Do you open it every day and read at least a verse, if not a chapter? I notice we don't have a Bible study group here, and that's something that needs addressing. But back to the main topic, Paul has been dealing with the comparative value of what he calls spiritual gifts. Evidently some people in the congregation were speaking in tongues; they asked Paul if that was cool; and bless his heart, he tried to explain. Now, Paul's not always at his best when he's 'splainin' things. I remember once coming across a reader practicing a lesson from Paul, asked how she was doing, and got back, "Oh Lord, St. Paul's been drinking again!" I find reading Paul a lot like listening to Stravinsky when the strings are at odds with the brass who are quarreling with the percussion who are not even on the same page as the woodwinds and chaos reigns, when all of a sudden he finds the major key and a grand theme and just lifts me right up off my seat. Paul's a lot that way. He's creating theology as he goes, and he has a good bit of trouble; but at times he just cuts it short and returns to proclamation where he has few rivals. The faith, hope, and charity passage—and the greatest of these is charity—is a masterpiece. So let's take each of those terms and ponder them a bit.

Faith. There's a word to conjure with. What is faith? What is faith to you? I know one thing it is not. Some Christians weaponize the word and use it to judge others. In a parish I served long ago, a young couple produced their first child, a son, and he was imperfectly made, mentally and physically, and lots of young parents would have surrendered him at once to some kind of specialized care. Not those two. They kept him at home, produced a little sister, and raised him; but the day came when he got to be too much to handle, and with great reluctance they surrendered him to an institution—whereupon another member of the parish said to them, "If you two had enough faith, that wouldn't have happened." Lord God! One of the cruelest things I ever heard. Let me tell you, that's not what faith is, not some kind of commodity you accumulate to fend off life's trials. I imagine everybody here knows that, and good for you.

When I think about faith, it helps me to compare and contrast it with belief, and in my vocabulary faith and belief are not the same. When I say I believe something, I'm speaking out of my Aristotelian bent which requires evidence and lots of it. I believe the world is round. Not everybody does. The writers of the Bible, lots of them, thought it was flat. They speak of the four corners of the earth and spot Jerusalem smack in the middle of it. Yet most of us don't believe that anymore. Not only is there its visible curvature in some places, but we also shot somebody up in space in a rocket ship to take a picture of it. It's round. I believe that. I believe that in fourteen-hundred ninety-two Columbus sailed the ocean blue and found this place. I believe it because there are written records in abundance. I believe that excessive heat applied to human flesh hurts. I set my hand down on a hot burner this week, and here's the visible evidence. When I believe, I believe I know. Faith is another matter entirely. Faith involves things I don't know for sure at all but about which I have what I might call a corroborated notion, a notion I got from someone else or fetched up out of my own experience and for which I have some, maybe a lot, of corroborating evidence, not the kind of evidence I can nail down but evidence I can nevertheless not deny. Know what I mean? I'll bet you do. I mean, I have faith that God is, but I can't prove it. Nobody can. Aristotle set out to. Thomas Aquinas thought he did. Yet every time somebody gets God all defined up, God just slips through the proof like quicksilver and goes right on being a mystery we cannot comprehend. Yet we apprehend God, we experience God, I for one cannot look at creation in its splendor and vastness and call it all an accident. I can't prove it, I can't quite say I believe it, but all that and a lot more gives me faith that God is. And so on from there. You follow, I know. And in Christian worship faith and belief sort of slip back and forth with each other. In a bit we're all going to stand up and say We believe in God the Father Almighty as an affirmation of our faith that God is.

Hope. There's another word with a variety of meanings. Sometimes we use it with some irony or vexation. Is so-and-so going to show up and do his duty? Well, I should hope so, which means I don't really expect it. Hope implies that something is in doubt, something at risk, a gamble going on somewhere. Hope can be the gritted teeth kind when we really doubt the outcome; and it can be the kind when we are pretty sure things are going to turn out well. There's a whole range of hope, and I'm still charmed by that word I picked up from Doug Hurd, *skeptimistic*, when we have lots of reservations but aren't quite ready to give up. When hope fails, everything else turns to dross, and if you've known hopelessness, you've known one of the heart's darkest moments. Just the same, when people are full of hope, they can endure the unbearable and smile. Hope, like faith, comes wrapped many ways.

Charity. Often these days the translators opt for another more general translation, *i.e.* love. Faith, hope and love. I sorta prefer the older translation. Paul was writing in first century Greek which had at least seven words for love—scholars differ on the exact number but never mind—whereas English has only one and then goes modifying it with adjectives—brotherly love, sensual love, the love we may have for a place or a painting of a symphony, divine love. Our word charity comes through Latin, and when we think of charity we think of something done to benefit someone in need, we think of Catholic Charities, and so the word takes on an active dimension. The original Greek word is *agape*, a kind of love that embraces all existence, reaches into infinity, seeks nothing in return, sets no limits or conditions. Agape love moves us to share ourselves and all we have without hesitation, to weep with the sad, to shout with the joyous, to feed the hungry, clothe the naked, visit prisoners, comfort widows and orphans in their affliction. All that. The kind of thing Jesus speaks of at the end of Matthew 25 when he rebukes those who never saw his face in "the least of these my brethren." The best meditation I know of on that kind of love is in Wesley's hymn, "Love divine, all loves excelling, joy of heaven to earth come down," the love that leaves us "lost in wonder, love, and praise." And, I might add, sends us out the door here to find Jesus in the face of everyone we meet.

I imagine by now you'll notice that those three virtues play back and forth among each other. Which comes first? Does either come first, or does one call on another in a mysterious interplay? Do you need faith to have hope which urges you to go to the world in love? Could be. I'm enough of an existentialist to believe that even if you have no faith, the act very of sharing, of sacrificing for the sake of someone else, affects us so that almost against our will we learn to be hopeful and finally find faith in the corroboration of Jesus' promise that giving carries a blessing of its own.

All right. Let's go back to the original matter. Our prayer affirms that we believe God promises us the kingdom. Jesus' parables say we are in the kingdom from the beginning. It's not something God withholds until we earn it; we're in it as a birthright, and the question in the parables is, who's the fool who gets himself kicked out? The best definition I ever heard of God's wrath is that the wrath of God is indeed the love of God as it is experienced by those who reject it. God gives us the kingdom, and we say Yes But. Know how God responds to that? When we say Yes But, God says, "Okay, have it your way. See how that works out. And when you get your eyes open again, I'm still here." Then he walks with us in the shadow until . . . well, you know. And as for the commands, I like to think more of God inviting us rather than commanding us, inviting us to share the splendor prepared for us from before the foundation of the world, brightening the earth about us and lifting us into that divine love which is ours from the beginning and beyond time into eternity.

Now quick quick, let's see if there's corroboration for that in today's lessons. We're finishing up a reading of Job, poor old thing, got the stuffing beaten out of him yet never wavered, and was rewarded with flocks and wives and children, in that order! What I like best in Job is his unshakeable conviction that, no matter what, God loved him. I know that my redeemer lives and that in the end I shall see God and not as a stranger! That's the kind of faith that carries you through the valley of the shadow. And in Mark, what does Bartimaeus ask for? Lord, open my eyes! Of course, the Bible often equates physical malady with spiritual rot, and we mostly think otherwise now; but as a metaphor, it works for us today. God, give us eyes to see the world as you see it, then to love it and serve it the way Jesus did. And Hebrews, that book so tied up in forms we find trouble relating to, today reassures us that when we fail, our failures are already forgiven in the perfect priesthood of Jesus whose sacrifice of himself was once and for all. Faith. Hope. Charity.

That prayer just about says it all, no? Oh God, fill us lip full of faith, hope and charity, so that loving your loving commandments we may be caught up always in your kingdom of love that surpasses all understanding.

Amen.

Simple stain glass windows run the length of the nave at head height. Since little is air conditioned in Cuernavaca, they open outward to let in fresh air.

1 November 2015

The Feasts of All Saints and All Souls

Wisdom of Solomon 3:1-9 Psalm 24 Revelation 21:1-6a John 11:32-44

Look what a gorgeous day God and his lady friend Mother Nature have given us to celebrate today's festival! I think it is wonderful for us to be here this morning with a house full of visitors, because simply by gathering to sing and pray, we become a kind of living proof of what this day signifies in the church's year of prayer. The Feast of All Saints is much like Easter, a day of pure proclamation. The church throughout the year remembers in prayer the great heroes of the faith, the saints whose names we recognize—St. Mary, St. John, St. Agnes, St. Clement, St. Catherine, St. Ignatius, saint saint saint. The list goes on forever, and they all have a day in the calendar when they are remembered and celebrated in prayer, the New Testament saints all in our prayer book. In our day we see the Roman Church adding new names right and left. In the Anglican tradition we don't exactly canonize people, but there's a whole list we call holy men and women whom we remember on specific days with prayers and lessons appointed. On this day, though, we take things farther. With audacious democracy, we claim sainthood not only for those great heroes but also we claim sainthood even for ourselves. That's a large claim, a claim of life and holiness in a world that often seems bent on self-destruction and unacquainted with holiness.

The very next day the church makes another large claim. The Feast of All Souls celebrates every single, solitary human soul who ever professed the faith of Jesus, from the days when he walked the earth right down to this red hot minute. Our prayers speak of a great cloud of witnesses whose names were never celebrated, the "folk like you and me" in the simple but powerful hymn we often sing on this day, people whose names time and tide have erased from history's memory perhaps, but not from God's. We also pray for those we, all of us, do remember—mothers, fathers, sisters, brothers, friends and lovers—who have crossed the bar and are seen no more, though in our own hearts and souls they are as alive as ever they were. I don't know about you, but I have a whole lot of friends on the other side I still talk to, and there are times when I get the notion they're talking to me. Here in Mexico tradition that goes behind the arrival of the faith of Jesus on these shores raises loving shrines to the beloved dead, celebrates their lives, eats and drinks with them, renews old loves. And what do we claim by all this? In a world that generally sees death as the end of things, we claim that at death life is not ended but changed, changed from glory into glory.

All this is splendid, isn't it? I rejoice in the splendor and light of it, and I know you do too. There is, however, something else here. These two feasts are clothed not only with splendor but also with a great solemnity; and I think we deprive ourselves if we do not deal with that solemnity. After all, what are we talking about here? Nothing less than life and death, those two great mysteries we all share. Here we are, alive and kicking and wanting to stay that way, yet we also all know that one day we too will shuffle off the mortal coil and that which came from out the boundless deep will turn again home. In the midst of life, St.

Paul tells us, we are in death, and a look at today's lessons drives that lesson straight home.

Those famous lines Mungo just read from the Wisdom of Solomon speak straight to our fear of death—it seems to many a punishment, destruction, the denial of everything we live and love and hope for. Yet, says the writer, we dare see things differently. We believe that death is not destruction but rather delivery into the hands of the God who made us, who will give us thrones of glory, will lead us into all understanding and grace and mercy, who will make us run like sparks through stubble. The God who loves us watches over his holy ones, his saints. That claim flies in the face of the culture of death and destruction. The psalm we read together affirms God's kingship over all and claims victory for all who strive to live holy lives worthy of the children of God. And the gospel. The raising of Lazarus is the final sign by which Jesus not only claims but shows in the flesh his power over death, his exhibition of a love over which death has no dominion. I can hardly read through it, because like a laser it reaches into the darkest depths of my soul and calls me forth, bound like Lazarus, into the light of faith and trust in God's unquenchable love for the likes of me. I wonder if any of you remember the Zefirelli film *Jesus of Nazareth*, came out in the seventies, all gorgeous and dramatic the way everything Zefirelli touched was. The setting of the raising of Lazarus was the sheer face of a great stone cliff, the kind they climb without anything to hold onto, straight up and down; to get to the door of the tomb, Jesus walked up a sort of ramp, growing tiny as he went until he reached the door, shouted the words of life—Lazarus! Come forth! A long pause and then the shrouded figure appeared, at which point the heavenly choir blew out the sound system with the "Hallelujah! Chorus." Pretty hammy, I know, but it worked! There it was, in the flesh, done. Powerful. Then the great hymn of victory from Revelation sees all our struggles ended and caught up in the mystery of Christ Jesus presenting his bride to the Father, and we hear the prophet's voice proclaim that God's habitation is with the mortals he has loved from the beginning, whose tears and cares he will wipe away forever as we are all caught up in him who is the beginning and the end, the alpha and the omega, our beginning and our end. Glorious all of it, yes, but glorious with a solemnity that puts us on our knees before we are raised in splendor. All these lessons speak straight to the eternal struggle between life and death, the way life has of teaching us to fear and doubt and turn in upon ourselves and each other because, for one reason or another, we like Eve and her compliant husband listen not to the God who created us for paradise but to the serpent who says, "God doesn't really mean what he says, you know." These lessons recall us to our first, truer nature and say that death is not the end of life but a part of life, a passage from this troubled world into a creation made new in the ever-renewing love of the loving God who made it.

Well now, there's the theology of these joyous feasts shorthanded the best your servant can do, because I want to move us on to happier ground. As is my wont, I'd like to turn our thoughts to that collect we all said Amen to when our worship began this morning, one of the most splendid in the church's treasury of prayer. Look at that opening metaphor. We thank God that he has knit together his elect in the mystical body of Christ our Lord. Don't fail to notice how fleshly this prayer is. Jesus often speaks of the way the faithful are bound up as one. He speaks of God's kingdom as a vineyard, says he is the vine, we the branches. St. Paul goes farther, chooses not a plant but our very own bodies, this meat we walk around in and are altogether too familiar with, and says we are the very flesh of Jesus, the Body of Christ, his eyes, his ears, his hands, his heart. In this meal we are about to share, we say we are fed with Christ's body and blood. How organic can it get? That language caused both laughter and scandal in the church's birthing days. People accused Christians of cannibalism, and you can see why, I reckon. Today's collect offers another, gentler metaphor. We are knit up—the language is Paul's—into Christ's mystical body. From my earliest childhood I have memories of women knitting, clicking and clacking those needles, pulling the yarn this way and that at amazing speed, turning out gorgeous shawls and comforters and booties and all that great artistry of love. I've known a few men who knit, though not many. Maybe more of us should. At any rate, the image is gentle and loving, just right I think for our celebration today of the love that winds in us and through us and all about us.

We also asked God for the grace to follow the blessed saints in virtuous and godly living. Let me assure you, virtuous and godly living does not mean trying very hard to be very nice. Oh, there's nothing wrong with nice, and I more than most could use some more practice at nice. But many if not most of God's great saints were far from nice. Was Paul nice? Poor thing, he rarely had the chance. He was pure energetic love in Christ, but he had a sharp tongue. I think of St. Leo, the bishop of Rome who stood down Attila. He must have been a pretty impressive guy. I think of St. Teresa of Avila, the great mystic whose passionate struggle with God all her life would have made her, to me at least, almost scary. And the modern St. Theresa of Calcutta—she hasn't quite got past the final barrier in the Roman process, but in her case, the church is playing catch-up—she was no nonsense whatsoever, often cut people off when they wasted her time, admitted openly that she had considerable trouble with faith. Saintly living goes way, way beyond nice. It's not a question of not drinking and smoking and playing cards and going to picture shows on Sunday and above all not saying bad words, that silly pollyanna kind of supersaturated niceness I remember hearing about as a child. Holy living means saying no to the cult of death and destruction which so often seems to be our true nature, our weakness, our foolishness, sometimes our wickedness, that nature we can neither explain nor deny. Holy living means more than that. It means all those things Jesus talked about at the day of judgment in Matthew 25, all that about loving the least, the last, the lost, the lonely, feeding the hungry and clothing the naked and . . . well, you know exactly what I'm talking about, and we can't have it put in front of us too often. What we do here is only the beginning of holy living; the validation of what we do here happens out there, day in and day out, a lot of it not one bit nice but all of it absolutely required for those who profess the faith of Christ. Holy living is a constant knitting up of the odds and ends of our varied lives, one act of love calling on another, one forgiven offense opening a door for love to heal, one sacrifice of self joining Christ's perfect sacrifice so our little world can be caught up in the restored creation glorified in God both now and forever. As the hymn reminds us, the peace of God is no peace but strife closed in the sod, and the call to holy living is a call into that strife. We answer it with fear and trembling but also with a smile on our face and a song in our heart, because we know how the movie comes out.

Such a cloud of witnesses surrounds us! What a glorious image that is. You who live up on the mountainside know the sense of mystery that descends when the clouds swallow you up. Today we hear a lot about how cybernetic information is stored in the cloud and that somehow means it is tick-a-lock safe where no one can break in and steal. Lean into that notion, fly to it when life is scary and you are weak, find strength and company for the road in the knowledge that countless souls have gone before you and are with you now, trudging forward to meet the bridegroom.

    Amen. Alleluia.

"I will wash my hands in innocence, and so shall I go about the altar of God." Unfailingly faithful acolyte Jorge Bredee grew up in Christ Church, Mexico City, and has served many priests at St. Michael's altar. The parish has a collection of handsome wrought silver altar ware, some encrusted with precious stones.

8 November 2015

Twenty-fourth Sunday after Pentecost

1 Kings 17:8-16 Psalm 146 Hebrews 9:24-28 Mark 12:38-44

I had the good fortune yesterday of meeting your fellow disciple Jim Papp, the artist who designed and created a great many of the lovely vestments this parish owns, including the hangings on the two lecterns and the chasuble and stole I'm wearing right now. I started bragging on his work, and he said, "Oh, they're about shot, especially that green set." Well, I begged to differ in the case of most of them; they look gorgeous to me; but I had to admit, this green set is a little faded. But it's no surprise, since green is the color the church uses most. It's called the "common" color, and we use it for the Epiphany season and for the long green season of Pentecost—which is, for this year, coming to an end. One more Sunday in green, and then it'll go back into the closet until next year.

Well now. That little exchange sort of set the stage for what the Church offers us for our prayers and our thoughts on this antepenultimate Sunday of this year's cycle of prayer. We're coming to an end, and the collect and the lessons are full of a sense of an ending. That phrase—a sense of an ending—is not mine. It is fact the name of a novel published some five years ago, but it wasn't original with the author. A good many of you here are either musicians or pretty interested in music, and you know that in general composers write in a specific musical key—think of this or that symphony in C or concerto in G—and usually start out in that key, then go wandering here and there through some of the other keys to create depth and beauty and excitement. But when the piece is about done, you usually know it, because the composer will linger dramatically in another key, often a fifth above the major and then bring everything to a close back in the home key. A narrative, a story or a novel, also often sends you signals it's about to end, works out all the kinks in the plot, ponders a bit about the road traveled, then ties a bow ribbon on it all and you're done. Ordinarily experiences tend to have, well, a beginning, a middle, and an end, and today's collect and lessons remind us that our Christian pilgrimage through life, already begun and still middling along today, will have an end—though that end, we believe, is in fact a beginning. (On that track, I thought mine was coming to an end Friday night. I had dinner with friends way south, got a cab back. The streets were rain slick, and the driver thought he was Mario Andrade. I lost my religion and found it again at least three times! The time is short!) We have a lot of work to do this morning, and I'm not sure I've got it all puzzled out; but I'm here to take a lot of it apart and consider it with you, and then we'll see what conclusions we can draw.

The collect begins with some scary language. We recall before God that he sent his son into the world to "destroy the works of the devil and make us children of God and heirs of eternal life." Already we are out in the deep end. That devil stuff, do Anglicans believe in that? What comes to mind at once, at least to mine, is the boogher man of my childhood, the medieval fellow with horns and a tail and goats' feet, all sooty and snarly, pretty scary back then, often a figure of burlesque when we're older and . . . know better. More recently thinkers like Dostoevsky have cast the devil as super suave and urbane, sly and insinuating instead of clownish, lurking in the dark recesses of our hearts. Well, whatever image comes to your mind, we simply cannot deny that the Bible is full of him, from the outset in Eden to the final visions in Revelation; and the collect speaks of his "works," which implies he's up to something. It would be comforting to ignore all that, and some do, but that would be risky. More in a minute. Going ahead, Jesus came to destroy those works and make you and me children of God—are we not his children by birthright, just by being born?—and heirs of eternal life. From there we can jump off into the theology of baptism, for one thing, and the undeniable fact that every human ever born has already died or eventually will die. So what's this about eternal life? But go on. When Jesus has done that, the collect says, we have hope, and since we have hope we are to "purify ourselves as he is pure," which carries us past the temptation to get sidetracked on morality and into the mystery of Christ's mysterious holy nature which, evidently, we can somehow obtain for ourselves. Keeping up? because we're not done. We then say Jesus will "come again with power and great glory" after which we will be "made like him in his eternal and glorious kingdom" which is beyond the reach of time and history. Wow. Loaded language. I haven't been able to learn when this collect was written, but as an English teacher I might ask them to pare it down a little. Nevertheless, here it is. And you said Amen to it.

We're not going to parse all the theology here, or we'd be here way past lunch, which God forbid! There is a great temptation here for me to escape into abstraction, into the language of myth and parallel and so on, a lot of English teacher stuff; but that would be cheap. I think most of you get the drift here. We're talking about the eternal struggle between what we call good and evil, between desperation and hope, between tearing down and building up, between the way the world sees things and the way God sees them, between life and death, all that. And we're talking about our hope, our belief, our faith that the God who made us has acted in the person of Jesus of Nazareth to lift us out of the muck and mire of so much of human existence and into the life of love and service Jesus lived and calls us into. Now just a whole lot of that is beyond us, out of our control for sure, so where is something we can get a grip on and maybe do something about? I think it's there in that part about purifying ourselves as he is pure, and the sixty-four dollar question is, purify ourselves from what? And once we decide on that, how do we do it?

Funniest thing, today's lessons show us three poor widows—the widow of Zarephath, the widow God lifts up in the psalm, and the widow who put everything she had in the alms box. I reckon it's a bit of a stretch for some of us to grasp the full weight of that persona. I mean, I've known some poor widows, I guess, but I've known a whole batch more who lived right well, all padded up with Social Security and 401Ks and investments and everything else their hardworking husbands killed themselves putting together, poor guys. Seems unfair from this side of the table. But we hardly have an idea of what being a widow was in the world the three we meet today lived in. Without a man to head the household, they were the outcast dregs of society, couldn't own property, could only beg; and if they had young children, so much the worse for the whole lot. Of course their brothers-in-law were supposed to take care of them, but there were lots of loopholes in that law. A poor widow was up the creek. You know, I got a real grip on that scene yesterday down in

Alpuyeca at the UTO ingathering. There were at least half a dozen little tiny *ancianitas* in the company, one in particular I remember vividly. The place was scrubbed so clean it squeaked, but she wanted to do something, contribute something, give something of herself. She peered in, spotted some speck of dust, maybe a gnat's wing, backed out, walked to the *bodega* and got a broom, shuffled back in and spent about five minutes batting whatever it was she saw until it suited her. She had all but nothing, but by golly she could sweep a little. And she did. But back to today's widows. What do they teach us about purifying ourselves, what were they free of that we need to learn about.

First, the widow of Zarephath, facing death from starvation during a drought, who just because Elijah told her to took the little she had and gave it to the prophet before she fed herself and her son. I could go on a long time with this story, but what I want us to see is what she was free of. She lived in bad times, bad for her, bad for everybody, yet somehow she never lost her trust in God's goodness, never gave in to the cynicism and hopelessness that often come over us. Sometimes we just give up hope—What can I do about it?—and at others we get mean—Get yours while the gettin's good! That kind of giving in can ruin a life. The widow may seem like a fool to sensible people like us, but when the time came, she took the famous leap of faith, right into the deep end of the pool. And swam. She was free of mistrust and fear. Are we?

Let's do Mark next. Jesus and the disciples are in the temple, watching the goings on. Some bigshots are paying their pledges with great flourish, and no doubt the Levites whose job it is to collect the loot are lavishing praise upon them. Jesus says, "Watch out for that bunch." And just then a little bent over thing takes her turn, puts in a couple of dimes, and shuffles off. Jesus says, "You know, those other guys, they could put in a hundred thousand, but they'd have millions left." Notice, he doesn't condemn their gift, not at all, just their attitude. Then he sees the widow. "This little thing put in everything she had. Now that's great." She was free from the love of money. Are we?

The psalm reviews that vision we got from the collect. The world is full of bad guys who live off everybody else, cheat and lie and steal and snatch and grab, and they oppress people who are weak and helpless and make easy targets for human predators. And though they think they get by with it, truth is, God sees every bit of it and he doesn't like it; and whereas those stinkers may go right on stealing and lying and so forth, God nevertheless loves and protects their victims. The psalm lists seven specific kinds of victims too: people who've been done in by the law, the hungry, prisoners, the blind, those bent over in body and spirit, those falsely accused, foreigners—and widows and their children. Not only that, God will hold them in his loving hand forever. There's sure an echo of the collect here. Those who learn to love God, God protects. Evil may seem to win, but it's an illusion.

Finally Hebrews again. I'll swear there are times when I just want to throw in the towel with all the contrasts between the old priesthood and the priesthood of Jesus. It gets a little too Platonic for me . . . but it sure deals with human appearance and divine reality, doesn't it? Today's reading turns a corner in the whole tale, says that Jesus' sacrifice has done once and for all what a thousand sacrifices of old could not do, namely deal with sin so we can get down to the business of becoming pure as he is pure to gain the salvation promised us from the foundation of the world.

Okay, take stock. These stories, especially the first two, show us people much unlike most of us—poor, powerless, on the outside looking in—and hold them up as examples we should follow, people free of doubt and fear and stinginess, free of the illusion that greatness lies in wealth and power and status. Though neither was likely much aware of it, those women were theologians who had figured out that greatness comes from God and only from God, and they lived their lives accordingly. They put no trust in things that in the long run would avail them nothing. You know the story maybe about the richest man in a little town. He died one night, and the next day, the place was abuzz with it. "Did ya hear? Old man Ledbetter died last night. How much do ya reckon he left?" The answer was, "Y'know, I believe he left it all." And we can't avoid the way these lessons have to do with things, possessions, wealth and the notion that we who have them should find them not a source of pride but rather a holy burden of responsibility and stewardship Jesus repeatedly calls us to share and share gladly. Each of us has to make up his own mind on all that, and a congregation has to make its mind up no less. I know some of you are involved in charity quietly, and bless you for it. I know this congregation is involved in some of that too, though I also know we can do better and before I leave I'll ask us to consider that matter pretty specifically, because the time is short. Philosophers and prophets tell us to live each day as our last, because you never know. It just might be.

Today though God gives us all time to take a hard look at the lessons, then turn that look inward on ourselves, individually and as the gathered family of God's children, made children because we try to follow Jesus. We know quite well we've got a good bit of purifying left to do. As we share Christ's body and blood at the table today, pray fervently for the purifying power of the Holy Spirit to wash us up, free us from fear and cynicism and greed and fill our hearts with so much gratitude that we can hardly wait to go out those doors and share the good news with the countless widowed souls we meet every day.

Amen.

Look at the colors! Pure Cuernavaca. When friends come to visit, I try to take them to Casa Hidalgo the first night they're in town. The balcony overlooks Cortez' Palace straight ahead and its small plaza. The main zócalo is to the left, always alive and entertaining . . . although in 2015 and 2016 it was undergoing major rebuilding, so our show was concentrated straight below us.

`15 November 2015

Twenty-fifth Sunday after Pentecost

Daniel 12:1-3   Psalm 16   Hebrews 10:11-14 (15-18) 19-25   Mark 13:1-8

As I began to think earlier this week about preaching to you today, I was so glad to realize that the collect for today is quite gentle, a little unlike some recently with all their complication and urgency about final things and so on. The prayer you said Amen to today is both a thanksgiving and a hopeful claim on everlasting life, which is a nice change. Although . . . it did occur to me to wonder why the folks who put the lectionary together decided to use it for this Sunday when the lessons are just as urgent as they can be. Whatever's the case, I'm glad for the chance to do a little teaching and then have a look at those lessons, because I think they actually suit the collect pretty well.

First, let's ponder the Bible a bit, the Holy Scripture we thanked God for causing to be written for our learning. Ever since Gutenberg invented the printing press, probably the single most consistent iconic representation of Christianity is a preacher with a Bible in his hand, often brandishing it like a sword, the Sword of the Word indeed! I remember when I was in seminary and doing hospital training in Fort Worth, I waltzed into a room and asked the bedded patient how he was doing. He said, "I'll be fine just as soon as I can get my sword!" I looked puzzled. "My Bible!" he thundered at me. The next day when I visited, he had a well-worn Bible on the bedside table. Christians then and very much today are characterized, like our Jewish forefathers, as People of the Book, and what a book it is. As I said in this week's e-mail message, I cleave to my ordination vow that I believe the Bible is the inspired word of God and that it contains everything we need for salvation, but I also know it's probably the most dangerous book in print. Ever since it became what it is some time in the fifth century, the Bible has been wrenched this way and that in a thousand thousand ways, depending on who's got hold of it, and has been weaponized and marshalled as evidence to justify some of history's most appalling horrors. If I mention the crusades and human slavery and the persecution of the Jews, I think that's enough of a list that could be extended. I neither want nor need to dwell on All That, because that's not what I'm up to today. That whole set of questions can't be dealt with in ten or fifteen minutes, and if you'd like to know some more about what I think about All That, check the e-mail Kay Godfrey will send you this week. I'll include something I wrote about All That a while back that pokes into some of the arguments. But I don't want to do that today.

Today, rather, I want to speak from my experience as a born skeptic who has spent more than half a century in a day-by-day tussle with Holy Scripture, as someone who denies none of the horrors I mentioned above and could mention a lot more, yet someone who finds that the longer I live with the Bible, the sweeter it gets. I don't think that's because I'm in my dotage, though God knows my mind wanders these days. I think rather that I've learned that it's no trick to pick this or that particular text to justify this or that particular human distortion of divine reality. That's easy, and the pages of history are littered with the victims of the murdering impostors who have done it again and again. Rather, sez I, we must look at the Bible whole, warts and all, and from its rambunctious wholeness tease out the mystical thread of God's view of us and all creation, God's way of revealing his loving and forgiving presence in a world that often seems utterly devoid of it. Living with the Bible that way takes work, frankly, and maybe it's wiser just to turn it all over to providence. Some people do, you know, and for them it works and I'm glad for them. But it doesn't work for me, and I suspect that it may not work quite so easily for a lot of you. God made me with a mind that, as Flannery O'Connor said of The Misfit, has to be into everything, and if God made me that way, then my grateful response to my Maker is to follow that restless mind through Holy Scripture until at length I touch the hem of the garment of God's divine glory. And at the risk of sounding mighty presumptuous, let me say that my search has not gone unrewarded, because I have learned from long dwelling with Holy Scripture to find corroboration of God's goodness almost everywhere I look.

Let me try to make this concrete. Today's lessons, all of them, deal with those end things we've pondered the last couple of weeks, what we commonly think of as the end of the world and what happens to us. But let me point out, the Bible is not the only place those end things get pondered. All the world's great religions and some of its perennial philosophies also deal with such things, and sometimes things don't turn out so hot. We don't have time for an exhaustive review of the literature, but let me talk about just one. Over at my little place, I don't have regular television, which is probably a good thing, since I'm an MSNBC junkie at home, need a break, especially at times like today when in some places it seems like things are crashing down all around us. Instead I've been watching lots of Netflix, and most recently I've been watching that wonderful series, *The Vikings*—pretty bloody but mighty instructive. Among its virtues is the way it brings Norse mythology to throbbing life with characters who really sure enough believed all that stuff and lived by it, no less than we believe the Bible and try to live by what it teaches. Norse religion is all about war, of course, since their God, not unlike ours often in the Hebrew scriptures, is a war god, and they are all about war and dying in battle and going to Valhalla to drink and carouse with their gods and chase women. But that's not quite the end of the story. Not at all. In that mythology, things go all haywire at the end, and the episode of the series that dramatizes *ragnarok*, the death of the gods, is pretty grim. It all ends up in flame and death and destruction, the absolute end of absolutely everything as a great snake swallows up the sun and dissolves into nothing. Pretty bracing, no? Makes me wonder, why try in the first place? To be fair, there is a kind of sequel where two people survive and repopulate the planet to start the whole mess over again. I still wonder why? That's not a narrative that appeals to me, though it is in some ways true to experience—the way life continuously surges, then perishes, then surges again. But in my view, it lacks purpose beyond the urge to survive. The story has no end, no purpose, no life of its own.

The Bible narrative is far more compelling. It includes a good bit of that concern for how things end, and today's lessons are all apocalyptic, about the end of time and history. Daniel's prophecy is as scary as the Bible gets, even has space ships that can go this way and that, and it would be easy to reject it for its sheer grotesquerie; yet at the end, what happens? At the end salvation and justice and goodness triumph. In this case St. Michael, our patron saint, brings it about, but the point is, it's a happy ending, an everlasting victory. The psalm is a paean to God's goodness and claims that at God's right hand are pleasures for evermore. Hebrews, after twisting and tossing and turning through an interminable exercise in comparison and contrast, claims the sacrifice of Jesus assures us that no matter how scary and horrible it all gets, our place in everlasting glory is certain. And the punchy passage from Mark is in the same vein. Remember, Jesus is with the disciples in the temple, the place where their religious upbringing tells them God Almighty dwells with men. The architecture impresses them, as architecture can. Christian architecture can be mighty impressive, as you all know, and we're like the disciples when our gaze turns upward in awe in some magnificent cathedral. Jesus, on the other hand, seems unimpressed. "Think this is something, do ya? It will all be knocked down." They understand that in light of their upbringing as the coming of a Messiah to restore the Davidic Kingdom, and they ask Jesus later when that will be. What does he say? "Never you mind about when that will be, because it's not a problem for you. Oh, there will always be people claiming this or that and saying they're God's appointed"—and how many false messiahs have many of us seen in our own lifetime?—"There will always be 'signs and wonders' and wars and earthquakes and all that. Never you mind. That's just the beginning of a new birth." That answer could leave a feller with questions, but what Mark's gospel does not say, the rest of the New Testament does: this life, with all its tribulation, does not end in death but in a birth into the life of God, not a recurring cycle of death and doom but rather a pilgrimage from history and its horrors into eternity and its splendor. The plenty scary book of Revelation, the great uncovering, ends not by starting all over again to repeat the same sad old story but rather with everything being caught up into the love of God from whom it all came. I have to tell you, my soul clings to that a lot more gladly than it could to a concept of reality as a vicious circle of death and destruction and darkness. The Bible story begins in darkness and chaos, but it ends in an endless expansion of God's glory in all things, including us. That is a story I can live with.

Needless to say, I can't prove a bit of it, wouldn't waste my time trying, don't think anybody can. What I do know, though, is that my own vision of what life and labor and love are all about is informed and shaped by what I believe the Holy Scriptures eventually reveal about God, what the Bible tells us if we learn to listen to it. The English teacher in me finds God's fingerprints in almost everything I read, no matter, because the Bible has given me a vision of life broad enough to encompass many many subsets of divine reality, has freed me from the need to corner God somewhere so I can understand him. Understand God? The notion to me is blasphemous. But to glimpse God everywhere, to find his glory everywhere, to know him in life's good and in life's horror, that's a way this pilgrim can find the courage to walk on. I thank God that Holy Scripture has shown me that path.

I don't know how many of you here read the Bible. I know you hear it read here in the gathered family, hear it preached by inadequate people like me. Maybe that's enough. I don't know. What I do know is that Christians need the Bible, need to nurse it to their bosoms, need to nourish themselves on its gnarly, knobby, difficult truths. If you do read your Bible and ponder it, God bless that to you. If you don't, dear hearts, when you get home, find your Bible. At least look at it! It misses you, and if you'll give it even half a chance, it will find its way into your heart with its abiding sweetness and wisdom. If you stay with it, I don't promise your path through life will be any easier, that you'll always find answers. The Bible often asks more questions that it answers. What I do promise you is this: the Bible, shaggy as it is, is man's best attempt yet to articulate that which words can only approach, the mystery of God's eternal love, and until we are all caught up in that glory, it's the best companion you can have on the way. I recommend it without reservation.

    Amen.

"And therefore with angels and archangels and all the company of Heaven . . ."

22 November 2015

The Feast of Christ the King

Daniel 7:9-10, 13-14 Psalm 93 Revelation 1:4b-8 John 18:33-37

  Today we join with millions of Christians of all kinds and all round the world to celebrate the last great feast of the church's year of prayer, the Feast of Christ the King, as we say Amen to that powerful collect about God's purpose to restore all things in Christ and free us from sin under his most gracious rule. It's a fairly new development in the liturgical kalendar. Pius XI instituted it in the Roman Catholic Church in 1925, in response to what he called growing nationalism and secularism. If you'll cast your minds back, you may recall that Pius XI had to deal with Benito Mussolini, so a response to nationalism and secularism was for him historically acute. At any rate, in a *Motu propio* he directed the feast be observed on the last Sunday of October, just before the older feasts of All Saints and All Souls, which we celebrated here three weeks ago. Pope Paul VI moved the feast to the end of the liturgical year in 1971, which is one of the happier decisions that poor fellow made. And as the great liturgical movement of the last century went forward, most traditional Christians around the world—Romans, Anglicans, Lutherans, Methodists, Presbyterians, some Orthodox—agreed that a year of prayer which endeavors to tell the old, old story of Jesus and his love would end quite appropriately in a festival in which the church rises up in joyous song to proclaim the reign of Jesus, as Pius XI put it, in our minds, our wills, our hearts, and our bodies.

  Well now. That's a large claim, isn't it? It's a claim I think we can risk making for ourselves some of the time. That we're here testifies to the fact that at least in some sense all of us claim citizenship in the Kingdom of God and his Christ, that to a greater or lesser extent all of us here strive to make Jesus Lord of our minds, wills, hearts, and bodies—though I think we'd all agree that we sometimes, now and then at the very least, fall some little bit short of that mark. I know I do, and I imagine you do too. And that's just little ol' us. When we look at the great wide world beyond, it's all very well for us to sing these magnificent hymns of triumph and proclaim that he is king of kings and lord of lords, while all around us history joins to drown us out as a world infected with greed and bigotry and violence and the love of money and a thousand thousand other deformations of God's goodness roars by on the fast road to Hell. Somehow one gets the notion that while the family of the faith of Jesus strives for and sometimes very powerfully knows the reign of Christ—God's kingdom come on earth—a great deal of the world seems to know nothing about it and to care less than it knows. One could get discouraged, many do, and in our day we see Christianity in apparent retreat on many fronts. At times it seems like the old collect for the twenty-fifth Sunday after Trinity would fit better. We used to call this Sunday Stirring Up Sunday for two reasons. First, the collect asked God to stir up our wills so we could bring forth the fruit of good works; second, the English tradition was to start stirring up Christmas puddings; both require a good bit of old fashioned physical labor. The fact is, this morning and every morning Christians find ourselves in that paradoxical already-but-not-yet condition of knowing where our faith is leading us, of seizing it from afar with the eyes of faith, while yet knowing ourselves surrounded by . . . well, the unredeemed world we live in and are part of, for better for worse.

Todays' collect and lessons take us directly to the heart of this quandary which is not only a quandary but also a great mystery. Remember, the collect says it is God's will to restore all things in his well-beloved son. That verb restore, now, what does that imply? That something which once was is no more, that something has been lost, that something has gone wrong and needs fixing. Well, you all have read at least the first couple chapters of the Bible, that book called Genesis, all that about the Garden of Eden, God's good and perfect gift to our parents, Adam and Eve. We all know that, perfect as it was at the outset—God scurrying around his creation workshop muttering Good! Good! Good! at every step—good as it was, things went wrong almost at once. That wrong had two parts, an outside influence and our cooperation, that lying serpent who said God didn't mean anything he said, and our folly in saying, You know, I believe you're right. All downhill from there, if you remember, and our blessed creator God shaking his head and saying, Okay, have it your way. Well, for way too much of our history, we've had it our way. The evidence is all about us. I don't have to hammer the point. We all know that somehow God's good purpose has been sidetracked; we also know that in many ways, a lot of the ongoing play out of that derailment is our fault, that we cooperate with it day in and day out, sometimes out of weakness and foolishness, sometimes out of downright wickedness; we don't like it, we don't understand it, but we can by no means deny it. We usually speak of this in what we call moral terms, good and evil; and those are terms laden with problems, but I fail to see how we can deny their reality. A great Christian thinker from Africa, Archbishop Desmond Tutu, has recently put it this way: "Theology has helped us . . . recognize that we inhabit a moral universe, that good and evil are real and they matter. They are not just things of indifference. This is a moral universe, which means that, despite all the evidence that seems to be to the contrary, there is no way that evil . . . can have the last word. For us who are Christians, the death and resurrection of Jesus Christ is proof positive that love is stronger than hate, that life is stronger than death, that light is stronger than darkness, that laughter and joy and compassion and gentleness and truth, all these are so much stronger than their ghastly counterparts." You and I, precisely because we profess the faith of Jesus, have signed up as combatants in that war between good and evil the archbishop names, and how many Christian hymns do we sing that ring with the imagery of warfare? Too many for my taste, but I have to admit they reflect the reality we are striving to face today and every day we live.

That's all pretty bracing, I know, and a little abstract. A look at the lessons today may help bring it closer to home. The dichotomy the collect presents leaps right off the page at us. The lesson from Daniel and the psalm and the lesson from Revelation are all couched in the language of triumph, of victory everlasting and final. Daniel: the one who is like a human, the son of man, comes from the clouds, is presented to the Ancient One, and receives a kingdom over all peoples and tongues, and that kingdom cannot be destroyed. Psalm: the Lord is king and that kingdom is not only for the future, it's been around since the beginning, everlasting, eternal, before and behind. Revelation: all eyes behold Jesus, even those who pierced him, and he is the alpha and the omega, the God who was and is and is to come, amen, alleluia, world without end. Wow. Notice, then, how John's gospel comes right smooth in the middle of all that, after Daniel and the psalm, but before John's great vision, and I'll be jiggered if it doesn't set up that paradoxical vision we explored just a minute ago all over again.

I've always felt a little sorry for Pontius Pilate. I mean, he was really on the spot, and according to the popular image and what little history there is to back it all up, he wasn't the heaviest hammer in the Roman tool box. He got sent to Palestine, after all, and in those days and that system, going to Palestine was not exactly like going to the Court of St. James today, not Paris, not even, oh, Riga. More like Mali, a real trouble spot, last place anybody with any sense wanted to go, a real career killer. Well, that's where Pilate is, and today's passage from John shows him in what we might call a mildly stressful situation. Duh. It's the highest holy day in the Jewish year, emotions are white hot as they always are in Palestine, and the priestly establishment wants him to make a decision about some guy making claims that make no sense whatsoever to him. They want a judgment and they want it now. I mean, what would you do? John, in fact, makes Pilate pretty sly. He's heard the charge, so he asks Jesus point blank, "Are you the king of the Jews?" He expects Jesus to say yes and make his job easy. For him, there is no king but Caesar who is indeed not only king but also emperor and a god to boot. As is Jesus' wont, however, he puts the question right back in Pilate's lap: "Where'd you get that? Do you think I'm the king of the Jews, or did somebody else tell you that?" Pilate cuts him off: "Look, don't quibble with me. I think all this is nonsense, but your own bunch has handed you over. What have you done?" Clearly he thinks in practical terms, what Jesus has *done*. That's where Jesus turns the conversation on its head. For him, it's not a question of what he's done but of who he is. "It's your question that's nonsense. I'm not like you, and if I were you'd have a fight on your hands. But my power is nothing like yours"—not of this world, are his words. Pilate cross-examines: "Aha! You say you are a king, then?" To which Jesus retorts, "Don't put words in my mouth. I am here as a witness to the truth, and people who see the truth know what I'm talking about." To which Pilate makes the comeback not in today's lesson, "What is truth?" Well, as they used to say, that's the sixty-four dollar question, isn't it? Jesus speaks right into the confusion between God's view of the world and mankind's usual view of the world, between man's idea of power and God's, one so violent and destructive, the other so quiet and upbuilding, between . . . well . . . good and evil, life and death. There it is again, and we who profess the faith of Jesus are right smack in the middle again: "Everyone who belongs to the truth hears my voice."

All right, that's enough, I think. We get the picture. So let's go back to the collect for that good part about being freed from sin and living under Christ's gracious rule. If you've been baptized, then in God's eyes you are already freed from sin and equipped for the battle of life, both now and on into eternity, because . . . well, what is Christ's rule? The same rule you've always known: love God with all your heart, soul, and mind, and love your neighbor just as much. We all know it by memory, know it so well it can pretty easily slide off our awareness like water off a duck or over a smooth river pebble. Maybe we should tattoo it inside our eyelids as part of baptism, because that and that alone defines everything else for us. The pope said he was asking the faithful to celebrate the reign of Christ every year to improve our minds, our wills, our hearts, and our bodies, and you know what? Those things can't be separated, because what we think affects what we feel affects our will affects what we do, and there's no pulling all that apart. Oh, I know there are people who try to divide the human animal up into discrete, unconnected realms, say that no matter how we live, if we think beautiful things, then we're beautiful too. A lot of New Age religion is like that. I have a friend, one of my dearest and closest, who flatly denies the reality of evil. Does anybody remember that song from the sixties? "Everthang is byoooootiful, in its own wa-a-a-ay," it went, and that's a right nice way to look at the world, I reckon, and for some people, it seems to work. Works for my friend. But as I've said to him quietly more than once, I think that view of the world requires a whole heap of denial. Yet the collect we all said Amen to says that in the long run, everything is indeed going to be beautiful. And you know? There's worlds of evidence for that too.

There's a fancy theological word that sums our condition up, and it's *proleptic*. It has several meanings, but one is a sense of falling forward, of experiencing something in the future as if it already existed, something that is already but not yet. Yes, that's a paradox, but living under Christ's rule in this world involves plenty of paradox, and you've been seeing it for years yourselves. You and I have all found ourselves doing things, saying things that make absolutely no sense under ordinary circumstances but doing them exactly because we're baptized. Things like feeding people who don't deserve help (the way the world thinks) or defending people who don't deserve it (the way the world thinks) or giving away our money, signing a pledge card, to an outfit that has no visible product (the way the world thinks) or forgiving people who have done absolutely nothing to deserve it (the way the world thinks). I mentioned Archbishop Tutu earlier. Well, he was a contemporary and collaborator with one of the greatest forgivers of the last century, Nelson Mandela, that amazing man who took it right in the face for years without complaining, who when he was freed from prison did not come roaring back in anger and vengeance but rather led a nation where white people and black people absolutely could not live with each other (the way the world thinks) to a place where they can not only live with each other but in fact work and build and love with each other. It may not yet be the Garden of Eden where he walked, but it is certainly quantum leaps away from the Hell it was when hatred ruled. I imagine you can think of a dozen other examples; I know I can. But I think we can do that at our leisure. Also at our leisure we can consider how to let our participation in the kingdom of God on earth, falling forward out of heaven, and our sure and certain hope of our citizenship in God's eternal kingdom can shape our minds and our wills and our hearts and our bodies from now on.

Right now though it's time to get up on our feet and proclaim our faith once more, to come to the table for nourishment, and to go our way rejoicing, knowing that this very day Christ will come to us in the face of someone who loves us and shares our hopes and our dreams for making the world a little more the way we know the Lord Jesus wants it to be. Find encouragement there. And Christ will also come to us in the face of someone cast out and cast down and hopeless and homeless and hungry and lonely. Pray that we recognize Christ in all those faces and turn none away. Inasmuch as we live according to that rule, we

live up to our call to be Christ's faithful soldiers and servants until our lives' end, in word and deed to profess the faith of Christ crucified, proclaim his resurrection and to share in his eternal priesthood, both now and forever.
    Amen.

Lay leader Ed Acker receives the Body of Christ. Chalicemen are Jorge Bredee and Carl Haymes.

6 December 2015

The Second Sunday of Advent

Baruch 5:1-9 Luke 1:68-79 Philippians 1:3-11 Luke 3:1-6

 As I step down into the aisle this morning, I am reminded of at least two songs. The first is "The Battle Hymn of the Republic," not exactly a favorite of mine with all its war imagery. The fourth verse, however, begins with the lovely image "In the beauty of the lilies Christ was born across the sea." I suppose if Jesus had been born in Cuernavaca, we'd need to change the flowers from lilies to poinsettias, as the fabulous display behind me attests. The other ditty that comes to mind is of more recent composition. I'm thinking of the 1951 Perry Como hit, "It's Beginning to Look a Lot Like Christmas." I expect you remember it, and here and everywhere as the feast of the birth of Christ draws near, the signs of that festival multiply in the public marketplace and in people's homes. Both here and in the United States, stores of all kinds have been banked with poinsettias and tinsel and colored globes since just after Hallowe'en. If I were at home I would have my crèche set out with the wise men perched a good distance away from the manger to remind me that Christmas indeed hasn't come quite yet. Today is the second Sunday of the Advent season, and we have a lot to ponder in this season of solemn yet joyous anticipation of things yet to come in which Dr. Howard Friend's sermon so winsomely located us last Sunday.

 When I came out of seminary back in the last millennium, everybody knew that Advent was not only a solemn season, it was in fact a penitential season. Bishop Barnds, suffragan of Dallas back then, echoed what everyone knew: Advent is a little Lent. How about that? Advent was a penitential season. I mean, why else did we put on purple vestments if we weren't doing penance, and everybody celebrated Advent in purple in those days. When I started using blue back in the 80s, I remember asking a lifelong Episcopalian how she liked the new vestments. Her arch reply was, "Well, they certainly don't make me think of Advent." Oh, it was solemn, make no mistake, and when I went as a young deacon down to Comanche, Texas, in 1966 I decided to teach them all about Advent's penitential caste, told them that among other things good catholic Christians did not have or go to parties during Advent. And for the first year, fool that I was, I thought they were obeying me. Then I found out, they were having parties all right; they just weren't inviting *me*. Since then the church has adopted a rather less stringent attitude toward Advent. Many parishes use blue this season, perhaps thought of as a lighter shade of purple, but also in honor of the Blessed Virgin's important role in bringing the light of Christ to the world in her baby. Some brighter Advent hymns and carols found their way into the newer hymnals. We just sang one before the gospel. The four classic themes to preach on the four Sundays of Advent used to be Sin, Death, Heaven and Hell. Nowadays they're more likely Hope, Peace, Joy and Love. All in all the whole season is lived with less emphasis on penitence and more on preparation, and I'm glad for that. It all seems a little more in keeping with the joyous news we will soon proclaim, that the Savior of the world has come as a babe at Bethlehem.

 For me a favorite way to pray and ponder in Advent, and I invite you to share it, is to contemplate what the world would be like without a savior, or a little more precisely, what the world would be like for me, for you, without Jesus. Keep in mind, the full revelation of the love of God in Christ Jesus happened only a couple thousand years ago; but the world, your ancestors and mine, were alive and living and loving and working and praying and dying for many, many millennia before that. What might it have been like then to live without the revelation of Jesus? And to pull that question up a little closer, I like to ask myself this: what would my life be like today without Jesus? I think that's a question everyone baptized in his name should consider now and then. How much difference does the fact that I am baptized into the life, death, and resurrection of Jesus make in my life right this red hot minute? It's a little hard to imagine, really, since most of us have been steeped in the awareness of Jesus from our mothers' knees. But it's worth a thought.

Today's collect and first lesson remind us of the world without Jesus, before Jesus, no Jesus. The collect that thanks God for the prophets who preached repentance to prepare for his coming, and Baruch's hymn of tip-toe excitement—God will show us splendor everywhere, the very mountains will be knocked down flat to make the road easy—both speak of something that is not yet. And in that realm we run into the figure who straddles the abyss between life without a savior and life with one: John the Baptist.

If we can believe Luke, Jesus and John were cousins, close cousins though whether first or second or third-down-from-the-longest-and-strongest double half cousins twice removed can't be established. John's the babe that leapt in his mother Elizabeth's womb when her youthful—and pregnant—kinswoman Mary came to visit her in the hill country. John's birth was not quite the bash Jesus' turned out to be, but his father Zechariah did break forth with a hymn of thanksgiving for the boy's birth that we sang just now.

By the time we run onto John again, he's about thirty and making a world of trouble, gone into the freelance propheting business—Israel's always worked alive with them—running around just outside the city limits, gathering crowds, and telling them: "Look here! This way! Turn around. Repent. Come be baptized to show your sins are forgiven. And look out, because the Kingdom of God is breaking in all over the place!" Well, that's what he said. Look it up. And he was not socially acceptable. He ate bugs and wore animal skins. A friend and I were looking at paintings of him once, and about one she asked, "What's that little critter he's feeding?" I had to say, "He's not feeding it. He's wearing it." That's the fellow who gets to be the first one to show Jesus to the rest of the world. God's thoughts are not ours.

A couple of things before we go any farther. First, the way we use the word repent. To us usually it means feeling very sorry for something we just got caught doing. There's nothing wrong with that as far as it goes, but that's only a minor subset of what the word actually means. The Aramaic word *shuv* that John used means turn smooth around and go the other way. Look the other way. The other way. Another way. John was asking people to forget all the superstructure of their religion, all the gesture and rite, all the sin counting, all the hope that God would soon ride in on a tall horse and vindicate them. "Forget all about that," he said. "*Shuv!* Turn around. Look the other way. Look this way!"

Second, some folks think John's the one who invented baptism, which is not even nearly so. The Greek word we get baptism from just means washing, and the Jews were big on washing up before they went to church. Remember: ours is a desert-born religion, and there's not a lot of water in the desert. The act of washing, part of the old holiness code, was in its origins very expensive, using up some of the rarest and most precious stuff they had, a real sacrifice. (To get a good sense of the holiness of water from a completely different context, see the first film version of *Dune*.) By the time John came along, of course, the Jerusalem religious establishment had all the water it needed, but they were still big on washing, baptism. Solomon had a vast basin of water, a kind of Holy Cistern, installed in the temple precincts to get the smelly masses scrubbed up. John didn't invent baptism, but he did use baptism as a sign of the forgiveness of sins. That was new.

Now, we customarily say John was the last of the Jewish prophets, though our Jewish and Muslim confreres don't agree. Today you heard from Baruch, another message of return and restoration, the children of Israel coming home from somewhere, coming back to Jerusalem, and so magnificent is that homecoming that the hills fall down flat so God's Israel can just stroll home on level ground. No rough places. Smooth sailing all the way. You heard it again when Luke's gospel quoted Isaiah. Now the fact is that both were talking about something quite specific: after decades of captivity in Babylon, the descendants of the first captives were coming back to Jerusalem. The King of Persia was paying their way home on first class tickets, and when they got there they had permission to rebuild their temple and go right back to the religion his royal predecessors had tried to blot from the face of the earth. And so the prophets at the time, watching and waiting and wondering, burst forth in exultant hymns of rejoicing and triumph. We're going home! And when we get home, we're going to rebuild the church house and start praying just like we used to, and then everything will be hunky dory. Since they were, in their opinion, the only people on the planet God cared about, they'd soon show the world How These Things Are Done!

Of course, that didn't happen. Things went from bad to worse. First this, then that, then the next invader conquered Palestine—Egyptians, Syrians, Greeks, Romans. By the time John showed up four centuries later, their religion had descended into a murky guilt management system which promised them that some day, by golly, God will take a hand and kick out all our oppressors and then we'll show 'em How These Things Are Done. No progress.

Now, if things were so bad off when John got the preaching bug, what on earth was he talking about? What prompted him to stand up and say, "Look here! Your sins are forgiven. The Kingdom of Heaven is coming upon you!" His predecessor prophets had the Persian king's amnesty to fuel their hope, but what on earth was John looking at? What drove him nutty, so nutty he risked his life with a bunch of foolishness about the Kingdom of God? It's for sure nothing was happening in history that could have encouraged him. The only conclusion I can draw is he was looking at the same thing you and I have been looking at for some time now: Jesus. I mean, the minute he got people looking his way and splashing in the Jordan and hoping for the Kingdom, the first thing he did was point away from himself and point at Jesus: "There he is. He's the one. That's the lamb of God. Listen to him." For the life of me, I can't imagine anything else that prompted him but Jesus—and I mean Jesus first-hand.

When I try to figure out John's motivation, I can't help recalling the cousins story. I mean, John had to know Jesus, had to know everything you and I know about Jesus and a whole lot more. He had to know that Jesus was really really different, really really onto something that would change history, would change the way people think and pray and live about and with God. All the sweetness and meekness and kindness and irresistible love, to say nothing of the Stand Up Guy Jesus who took on the most powerful people in his world without hesitation, John had to know about, had been drawn to, had talked and prayed and argued with. That's what young people do, especially earnest young people working out the way they live with God. And years of such spiritual 'rassling with Jesus had convinced John that . . . well . . . what he said: "There he is. Jesus. He's the one. Listen to him."

I think Jesus re-draws the picture of God and does that just by being himself, who he is. We believe Jesus is God incarnate, that God loves us so much that he became one of us—which is scandalous to many—and that when we look at Jesus we see God whole, all of God. And who, what is God? God is love. That's a word that'll slip out from under you if you're not careful, but let's specify at least one critical aspect of God's being that Jesus announced, lived, was: self-sacrificing love, self-denying love, self-abnegating love. You first love. Me last love. The kind that even the Baptist embodied when he said of his cousin, "That's the one. I'm nobody. I will vanish. He's first. I'm not worth taking his dirty shoes out to clean." The kind of love that in simple terms says, "You first, me last." I've noticed something on this visit I hadn't noticed before, the incredible courtesy drivers, most of them, show each other in Cuernavaca. If there's no traffic light at a busy intersection, drivers wait for each other, you let me by this time, I'll let you by the next. A simple sign of the kind of love Jesus lived that runs from there all the way to, "Here, kill me and leave them alone" in more challenging moments when someone lays down his life for another. Now that was new. Isaiah talked of the Suffering Servant; Jesus was that love. That's one.

Another, I reckon, was the revelation that the way God wants us to serve him is not chopping up livestock on an altar but rather going to the last the least, the lost, the lonely, the least of "these my brethren" and giving them the shirts off our backs. Literally. That's new. Amos warned about mistreating the helpless; Jesus was one of them, lived with them, sought their company.

And another. With the baptism John preached, Jesus shows us that God is not mad at us, indeed that God loves us so much that he's somehow overcome, forgiven, all the weakness and foolishness and wickedness and sloth we slosh around in most of the time. John's baptism was not a trick, not something to do so God would do something else. Baptism, Christian baptism, is not the way we elicit a Pavlovian response from God: We don't baptize to get God to do something; we baptize because God has already done something. And that was new. Even more amazing was Jesus' promise that when we live baptized, forgiven lives and clothe ourselves in that self-sacrificing love that feeds hungry people and loves people who aren't worth shooting, when we do that Jesus binds us to himself and promises that where he is we will be. With him. Forever. Jesus is a walking RSVP invitation to life in the Kingdom of God. Is it any surprise John had to tell somebody?

So this Advent, let's ponder the Baptist a little, and let's give thanks for his knowledge of Jesus, for the love that made him say, "Not me. That one." And let's thank God for the forerunners who showed Jesus to us. Your walk with the Lord may have started at your grandmother's knee; it may have started in a brawl in a saloon; it happens all over the place, all the time, right this red hot minute. There is a world not forty yards from where you're sitting that knows very little about Jesus, lives in a boiling kettle of anger and fear and frustration and violence, and does that world ever need somebody to point it to Jesus! This Advent ask St. John to fill you with his excitement, fill you so full you can't keep quiet about it. Hope for the day when you can be the one who shows Jesus to someone worse off than you are, when you can be a strange sign post in the desert of somebody's thirsty soul. Maybe you've already had that blessed chance. If you have, do it again. And if you haven't, as the Advent prayers teach us, be alert, be aware, keep your eyes open. Some day, somewhere, you'll be the one whose turn it is to shout, "Hey! Look here! You've got options. Forget all you've heard about how bad you are, how useless life is. Your sins are forgiven. And look at that one, Jesus, the Lamb of God. He's the one. Listen to him!"

Come, Lord Jesus.

Amen.

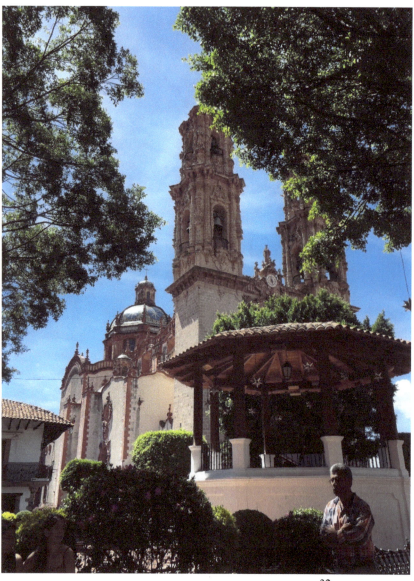

Fabled Santa Prisca Church dominates the tiny plaza in Taxco, an hour or so drive south from Cuernavaca and up into the Taxco Mountains. In the eighteenth century the silver mines in Taxco produced most of the world's silver and made the Borda family immeasurably rich. The family lived, however, in Cuernavaca where their palatial dwelling and gardens are a tourist attraction today. In 1750 José de la Borda ordered the church built for the use of the miners and their families. The interior is breathtaking, makes you think the Kingdom of Heaven is falling from the skies. It is still a parish church used by high and low alike.

13 December 2015

Third Sunday of Advent-*Gaudete*

Micah 5:2-5a Psalm 80:1-7 Hebrews 10:5-10 Luke 1:39-55

It will not have escaped your notice that the candle on the wreath we lit today is pink, whereas the other three are blue, would be purple in some places. There's a reason for that, as you might guess, and here it is. The third Sunday of Advent means the season is half over, that the solemn though not penitential character of our worship as we approach Christmas will end in less than two weeks as the church wakens in the night to the sweet, joyous news that a baby has been born. So as a sign of that, the color for this Sunday is neither purple nor blue but . . . pink. Well, it's usually called rose, but the fact is, that candle is pink. So are the vestments I should be wearing today if I were following the rules, and this parish has a lovely set of pink . . . ah . . . rose vestments; but pink is just not my color, so I am wearing these which have lilies embroidered to honor our Blessed Lady the Virgin Mary. Which leads me to the second reason this third Sunday in Advent is special.

I think I agree with most of what the reformers of our lectionary, the Bible lessons we read Sunday by Sunday, have done, almost all of it. But one thing I do not understand. For centuries, the third Sunday of Advent focused our attention and our prayers on the role of the Blessed Virgin in bringing Christ Jesus into the world, just as the second Sunday focused on the prophetic role of John the Baptist in calling the world's attention to his younger cousin. As John's day is the quintessential day of prophetic call, Mary's day was the quintessential day of the believer's humble response to that call. And for reasons of their own, the reformers gave us not one but two John days and pushed Mary to the last Sunday of Advent. Well, I don't like it, so here in this parish, we're celebrating Mary on the right day, the day we light the rose candle, the Sunday whose name is *Gaudete*, the Latin for Rejoice! I like it better, and God knows that here in Mexico where yesterday was the feast of the Virgin of Guadalupe, this is the right time to do it. I mean, the fact that Mexico's patroness is celebrated on December 12 is no coincidence: December 12 is always going to fall near the third Sunday of Advent. So there we are. That's why I read next Sunday's lessons this morning. This morning I call you to consider the maid from Nazareth who became the Mother of God.

You are all familiar with the story, first from Matthew, then in far greater detail in Luke. You just sang it in that gorgeous Advent carol the choir led so beautifully. The Angel Gabriel visited a maiden—a little girl no older than fifteen and presumably a virgin—and told her she'd have a remarkable child. She demurely inquires how that may be, considering the circumstances, and the angel tells her the Holy Spirit of God will engender the child, and apparently that is enough for her. It is God's will and God's doing, so she bows her head and submits: "Behold the handmaid of the Lord. Be it unto me according to thy word." And that, as they say, was that. Not only do you know the story, you've seen countless imaginative illustrations of the moment, all the way from ancient mosaics and frescoes to works by the greatest European painters right down to movie representations. And in almost every case, the angel looks a little sappy—or a little scary as in the carol, "his eyes as flame"—Mary is often seated at some kind of needlework as a well-brought up maid might be, and it is all just as sweet and ordinary as a caller at High Tea. Right?

Well, all I can say is that from that day to this, no figure in the gospel story other than Jesus himself has been the subject of greater adoration and devotion or attracted more attention, not all of it favorable, than that little girl. Though once Jesus grows up she fades into the background of the scriptural narrative, from the earliest days of Christian history there has been a vigorous urge to pull her out of the shadows and shower her with praise, endow her with special powers, and that urge continues to this day in the Roman Catholic Church where she has been declared born free of sin, assumed bodily into Heaven, and in considerable danger of being declared co-mediatrix with her Son. Lord, understanding one mediator is hard enough for me, and for the life of me I can't see the need for another. But there we are. I'd like to spend just a little time on that controversy.

First, the Christian religion has no monopoly on the notion of a miraculous birth, a child divinely engendered. Just Google up virgin birth in mythology and you are presented with more than you want to read, some of it simply descriptive—telling you about the literally dozens of virgin births in dozens of mythologies—to the violently combative—people arguing that the whole notion is ridiculous to people crying Blasphemy! in beet red prose. The whole notion has been a problem for Christians from the outset, and a great ping-pong game of affirmation and denial can be found in Christian literature down through the centuries. Back in the 1920s, a rector of Trinity Church where I sit on a pew at home allowed at some point that it was possible to doubt the virgin birth, and the preacher at the First Baptist Church, J. Frank Norris, threatened to shoot him dead on sight. I have no intention to take us through that theological mangrove swamp. Rather let me tell you a story. Back in the late 1960s, Michael Ramsey, the one hundredth Archbishop of Canterbury, led a conference of the clergy of the Diocese of Dallas which yours truly attended, a very young priest then. The topic was something like "Christ in the life of the church," I forget what exactly, and the old man was brilliant, had us all spellbound. At the end of the third day, he asked for questions. Most of us tried to sink into the floor, wouldn't dare ask him anything. All of us, that is, but one. There's always one. Another young priest, really bright but really full of himself, stepped forward and said something like this: "Michael"—yes, he used his first name—"Michael, I have found these lectures truly wonderful, but I am very sadly disappointed that you have said almost nothing about the importance of Christ's mother, the Blessed Virgin, in all this. After all it is the virgin birth that validates and proves everything Jesus ever said or did." Something like that. We all sank further into the floor. The archbishop paused, his great shaggy eyebrows waggling, and then replied very gently and ended up with something like this: "After all I don't think it is the virgin birth that validates or proves anything. Rather I believe that Jesus' whole life, his teaching, the signs he performed, his trial and death and resurrection, all that which make the notion of the virgin birth *just plausible.*" Just plausible. This from one of the greatest Anglican theologians of the last century. Now that's the best I've ever heard anyone deal with the whole unresolvable question, and I think I'll just leave it right there. You can, if it bothers you, make up your own mind.

I'd like to turn now to what I'd call the human side of this story. Leave the theology and mythology and all that aside, and let's just think about that little girl, Mary of Nazareth. She was fifteen. Fifteen, mind you, no older. She was evidently from a good family. Tradition has it that her parents were Joachim and Anna, though the Bible doesn't mention them. She had been raised in the Hebrew tradition of her time where young girls were married off by their fathers to suitable husbands, suitable both as good Jews and as good providers, and her father had promised her to a man named Joseph, a carpenter. It was simply assumed that she was chaste. Her prospects were quite good. And then something happened. She turned up pregnant, although she swore she had been a good girl. Can you imagine her mother when she figured it out? Mothers of fifteen year old girls watch those matters like hawks. I know. I raised two daughters. And can you imagine the scene when Anna told Joachim? I can imagine how I would have reacted, believe me. Who is he? Who did this? Frothing at the mouth. Nobody? A likely story! You tell me right now or . . . Well, you get the point. Mary was what we used to call in Montague County a little girl in trouble. Well, Joachim went to Joseph and offered to call it all off, but Joseph said he could live with it—another angel intervenes in the scriptural story—and the marriage was on. Quickly. She goes off to visit her cousin in the hill country to get her out of sight, because you can be sure there was talk. Then before she delivers, she has to ride a donkey across hill and dale to Bethlehem for the census and delivers that baby in a livery stable with no help, surrounded by livestock and draught animals. If there's a miracle involved, it's that she or the baby survived the birth. After that, she and her husband had to leave the country to avoid religious persecution, and when they came back and settled in, you can bet Nazareth hadn't forgotten a bit of the scandal. That's what it was like for Mary. Saying Yes to the will of God got her into more trouble than most of us can very well imagine. And yet . . .she stuck with it. She doubted her son at least once, we're told, but she stuck by him. At the last only she and Mary Magdalene and another Mary stood by him, though John claims he was there too. The rest of her story is purely traditional, though the tradition is strong. She lived with John at Ephesus where she died, greatly honored by the Christian community there. And the rest is history.

What I come away from all this with, and I offer it to you, is that it makes absolutely no difference whatsoever to my commitment to Jesus whether his birth was this way or that. I am not like the Jews, I don't seek a sign. I don't need a sign, because I know the *man*, and I am convinced through and through that he incarnated God's immeasurable love and power wholly, as least as much as I can handle, more than I can handle. How God accomplished that is, for me, God's business. My business is to see it and believe it and love it and worship it and obey it with all my heart and soul and strength and mind, so help me God. Once I've said that, all the rest sort of falls into place, and I have no problem whatsoever taking Mary as a model and a friend and an intercessor. She is the model of humility and submission to God's difficult will. She is friend to all who are at times confused and afraid. She is an intercessor whose prayers I have no trouble asking for. After all, she was Jesus' mama, and who knows her son better than a Jewish mama?

As we come soon to celebrate Jesus' birth, most of the world still lives in fright, still wishes for delivery, groans, in St. Paul's image, like a woman in childbirth. We will gather in the still of the night in the beauty of holiness to sing songs which make us feel wonderful and adore the sweetness of the incarnation. What is more wonderful, more joyous? Yet we must not come for the sweetness of it alone but also to hear the awesome majesty of the archangel's call to each of us to let our souls, like Mary, be the Christ's earthly sanctuary. As he was born of her, so must he be born of us. Mary brought her baby to the world at his birth. We must bring him to the world all the days of our lives. Birthing babies, they tell me, is hard work, so when you come to God's altar in the dark, ask the Virgin to ask God to help you take up for all your days the sweet work of showing God's wonderful son to all the fearful, confused, uncomforted, yet hopeful world.

Holy Mary, Mother of God, pray for us sinners now and at the hour of our death.
Amen.

Senior Warden Sandy Acker greets the preacher at the back door.

24 December 2015

Christmas Eve

Isaiah 9:2-7   Psalm 96   Titus 2:11-14   Luke 2:1-20

Of the Father's love begotten, ere the worlds began to be,
He is Alpha and Omega, he the source, the ending he,
Of the things that are, that have been, and that future years shall see,
Evermore and evermore.

Those opening lines of one the most splendid hymns in the collection (Hymnal #82) we will sing on one of the Sundays yet to come in the Christmas season this year. A beautiful, soaring melody, this hymn deserves our notice for more than its musical beauty. It contains a truth about the festival of the incarnation which can make this season both lovelier and more awesome to each of us as we celebrate tonight and for the next twelve days the birth of the Blessed Child.

The little boy whose birth we celebrate tonight, Jesus, has two names—Jesus and Christ—and they are significantly distinct in theology yet fused as one in our common speech. Christ has always been. Jesus has not. Christ is Alpha and Omega, has been since before the worlds began to be, from all time. Jesus was born one night in an obscure village in Palestine two millennia ago. The eternal separation of the two and their eternal union contain within that paradox the mystery and the great joy of the message of Christmas. We are asked tonight to ponder, ever so briefly, the mystery of the incarnation of Christ in Jesus, our Lord and Savior.

God the Son—the Christ—has been with the Father always. Nobody was standing around taking pictures when God articulated himself into three persons, as Christians believe he did, or when he first began to create the cosmos which we know and live in. All we know by faith is that God has always been and always will be. That's what we mean when we said "World without end" at the end of prayers for centuries—or "Now and forever" as we say now. It is a misconception to think that, on that first Christmas night in Palestine, there was a change in God. God does not change, doesn't have to, since he is perfect and complete in every way. The Son of God, which is what we usually call the second person of the Trinity, was already alive with the Father when Mary gave birth. He had been around always, and he had been busy. St. Paul thought he was the rock that followed the Hebrews in the wilderness. St. John said he is the light which lightens all men—and that means that any person in any age in any place who is enlightened is enlightened by Christ, before or after the event at Bethlehem. Romans takes note that good men in all times have sought God and known him. The nature of God did not change that night. Rather God in his own good time chose to reveal that nature anew to his chosen people and to all men of good will.

Jesus of Nazareth was a baby born in a place on a night, largely in the ordinary way. Two things—among others—make that birth notable. First, it overturned completely the expectation of the people of God about what the messiah, the anointed one, the Christ, would be like. Instead of a military genius who would throw out the Romans, kick the

Persians in the teeth for good measure, and reestablish the political ascendancy of Israel, God sent a baby. A great disappointment for those who, though they had ears, could not hear the angels' message of good will to all men. After all, the only thing babies are good for is loving on, and that was not in the standard job description for the messiah. The second thing was that the little tyke had a split personality. He was a normal little boy who wet his swaddling clothes and cried for his mother when he was hungry and generally was a lot of trouble. He was also God the Son, eternal, begotten of his Father's love before the worlds began to be, the redeeming revelation of God's eternal goodness and love—right there in the manger, little bitty, helpless, wiggly, limber-necked. This is not to say that the infant Jesus was lying in his baby-bed thinking, "I'm going to be the Savior when I grow up." It means something far more wonderful than an unusual vocation for the son and heir.

The split personality, you see, was not really split. In that one body dwelt not a naughty human soul and a very, very good divine spirit, but rather the union of all that humanity is with all that God is. In Jesus who is Christ, God acted in love to restore his own beloved and truly beautiful creation to himself—created in love in the first place, sustained and taught and led in love in the second place, and now wholly united to him in love in the final revelation of his own splendid perfection. What a surprise! All through the history of the Old Testament, God had this one up his celestial sleeve while we and the rest of our race had run hither, thither, and yon, trying first this and then that technique for propitiating him to our side—when all the time what he wanted was to be one of us so we could be his. The astonishing way he chose to accomplish that—causing a birth (which is not at all out of character, since he's been in the creation business all along)—makes this festival of ours at once sweet and mysterious, both delightful and overpowering. In that birth, that most common of human experiences, God Almighty broke down all the barriers which for all time had separated the creation from its maker. A birth, simple as that, though we should know by now that when God means to get something done, he doesn't fire off volcanoes or earthquakes or send plague and pestilence. Rather he brings off a birth. Lucky us who live in the blessed aftermath of that most blessed birth. Blessed we indeed who can gather peacefully and in holiness in the quiet of the night to celebrate that moment when, as the world lay in darkness, the divine light leapt among us, forever to be ours—as another great hymn says (Hymnal #91).

Break forth, O beauteous heavenly light,
And usher in the morning.
O shepherds, greet that glorious light,
Our Lord a crib adorning.
This child, this little helpless boy,
Shall be our confidence and joy,
The powers of Hell o'erthrowing,
At last our peace bestowing.

I wish for you all a blessed Christmastide, filled with joy and peace and the gently overpowering love of our Father God who sent our brother Jesus to be Christ in us.

Gloria in excelsis! Alleluia! Amen.

27 December 2015

The First Sunday after Christmas

1 Samuel 2:18-20, 26 Psalm 148 Colossians 3:12-17 Luke 2:41-52

Well, finally! Finally Christmas belongs to the Christians again. As no doubt you've noticed, ever since Hallowe'en the great world around us here in Mexico and certainly in the U.S. and Canada and just about everywhere else has been celebrating Christmas with an urgency born more of a certain mercantile impulse than of any particular piety. Of all the seasons of Christian prayer, Christmas is certainly the most popular. People who rarely if ever set foot inside a Christian church run themselves ragged buying gifts and throwing parties and asking each other if they're ready for Christmas, and goodness knows yours truly has enjoyed his share of the festivity. While here at St. Michael's, we've done our best to keep a holy and cadenced Advent season and are just now starting our twelve-day observation of Christmas, for most folks it's history, over and done—and, as they say, thank God it only comes once a year! I remember when we lived in Cleburne, I could stick my head out the door of the rectory on St. Stephen's day and see the cadavers of withered Christmas trees on just about every front curb except ours. Well, whatever. All I know is that Christians of catholic heritage will be celebrating the birth of the child and singing Christmas carols from now until January 6 next year when in good time we will recall the visit of the Magi to the manger at Bethlehem. We are in no hurry to bring it all to a close.

Aside from lamenting the way so many seem to go a little loony as Christmas nears, I've spent some time over the years pondering just why it is, of all the Church's proclamations, Christmas is the one that appeals to so many, almost to everyone, no matter whether they are Christians or not, and I think I have an inkling. What we celebrate at Christmas, after all, has to do with some of life's most fundamental and universal experiences—birth and the joy of new life, long-forestalled hopes fulfilled, the goodness of family and friendship and fellowship, the longing to belong and feel loved and prized, the joy of giving of ourselves in so many ways, the comfort of deliverance from whatever demons beset us. There's a lot involved in Christmas that touches just about anyone, so I guess we shouldn't be surprised to see all sorts and conditions of people joining us in their way as we gather the Christian family around the altar and around tables in all our homes. I could only wish that . . . well, if wishes were horses we'd all have a ride. I'm just glad that now we have a few days in the Church's life of prayer to ponder what all this fuss in fact means to us, how the yearly remembrance of the birth of Jesus changes our lives.

The collect you said Amen to and today's lessons teach us a lot. The collect thanks God for once again pouring the light of Christ into our lives, then asks God to let that new light enkindled in us shine forth in our lives. That's not difficult, is it? We receive the grace of the light of Christ daily, and our response is to let that light be seen in us by others. Then we have that charming passage from I Samuel. The child Samuel has been turned over by his parents to serve the old priest Eli who's gone blind, and every year his mother, who surely missed him, made him new clothes and brought them to him, because the boy was growing, the way they do. The story in Luke's gospel picks up the same theme. Jesus is big enough to get lost; he's growing up. If you have raised children, I expect you remember the first time one of yours got lost. I sure do. Ginna just didn't come home from school one day, and I promise you panic reigned in our house until, thank God, we found her not two blocks away, going about her business which was playing with some of her friends. So it was with Jesus' parents who found him going about his business, and as the first lesson said of Samuel, the gospel says Jesus grew in wisdom and in stature and in favor with God and men. The point is, both Samuel and Jesus started young and unfinished, but both grew. I think the lesson the lectionary is offering us as Christians is that we too must grow, that the new beginning we make each year at this time must be nourished and tested and put to work, we must get about our business. And what is that business? Samuel's was to take care of Eli; Jesus' was to begin to learn of his Father's business; ours, what is it? Colossians so gently reminds us. "As God's chosen ones, holy and beloved, clothe yourselves with compassion, kindness, humility, meekness, and patience. Bear with one another and, if anyone has a complaint against another, forgive each other; just as the Lord has forgiven you, so you also must forgive. Above all, clothe yourselves with love, which binds everything together in perfect harmony. And let the peace of Christ rule in your hearts, to which indeed you were called in the one body. And be thankful. Let the word of Christ dwell in you richly; teach and admonish one another in all wisdom; and with gratitude in your hearts sing psalms, hymns, and spiritual songs to God. And whatever you do, in word or deed, do everything in the name of the Lord Jesus, giving thanks to God the Father through him." My oh my. Does that describe the way I behave? I fear not, not all the time to be sure, and yet it could hardly be clearer, could it? And that prescription is just the beginning from which this little child in the faith is supposed to grow up into the fullness of Christian maturity. I've been a Christian, at least in name, all my life, except for a little while when I was in college and was too smart to be a Christian. But at least since I confirmed my baptism in 1961, I've been a professing Christian. You'd think I'd have it down by now, but I often feel less like a grown-up and more like little Samuel, needing to change his britches every year. Do you share some of that? If you have a conscience, I suspect you do, and if you don't, I recommend you give it some thought. Well, I won't belabor the point except to repeat: our Christmas celebrations are a renewal in our hearts and lives of the light of Christ. The way we let that light shine from within us is the proof of the Christmas pudding.

 All the foregoing is, of course, highly personal, depends on each of us in our spiritual walk day by day. I also want this morning to point our minds a little toward our responsibility as a Christian family, as members of a Christian congregation, the Church. As most of you know, I'm an English teacher, so I can hardly miss the opportunity to look beyond the Bible to what is, outside Luke's telling of the tale, the best known fable about the birth of Jesus. I mean, of course, Charles Dicken's *A Christmas Carol*. I can hardly remember when I wasn't aware of that splendid story of the way the light of Christ came to Scrooge, certainly one who walked in darkness and the shadow of death. You know the story as well as I do, and we've all read it and seen it acted again and again. You will recall then that before he sends Scrooge to lavish his newfound generosity on the Cratchitts, the Ghost of Christmas Yet to Come pulls back his great, glittering cape to reveal two "wolfish" children crouching there. Their names are Ignorance and Want, and they are dangerous. The ghost warns Scrooge that until those children are loved and cared for, no one is really safe. There's a message there for us. What about our witness to the gospel has failed to dispel the Ignorance of the God of love that rages about us like a roaring and a ramping lion, seeking whom it may devour? What, I ask myself, have I not said, done, prayed, to roll that Ignorance back? What in the witness of this congregation, the Anglican Church, the whole body of Christ in earth must change to overcome that hot Ignorance with the love God entrusts us to share with those who know him not? And in the Want department. As I walk or am driven around this gorgeous city and enjoy the hospitality, I can't help seeing on all sides that there are some folks among us who aren't having a very Merry Christmas, very rarely have nice day. What have I not done, said, prayed that keeps Want's numbers growing? What can I, can you, can St. Michael's Church, any of us who say we love God do to find the right way to feed, clothe, shelter, comfort Want? I know many here are involved in one way or another with obeying those commandments, though we too often get bogged down in the method. I have been so proud to see your response to some needs I've laid before you, and I urge you to redouble those efforts, because what I know is, we've got to be about it, and until we are, we've got no right to celebrate our own blessedness. And on that cautionary note, I think I'll let that matter rest with you and your own growing up in the faith.

Now let's finish saying our prayers, and feast at the Lord's table, and then go home to our own families, our children and mothers and fathers and all those we love. It's only right. And while we're there and for every day of the Year of Grace to come, not just the six crazy weeks before Christmas, not just for show, let's keep in mind the world Jesus came to, including those scary kids, Ignorance and Want. Cuernavaca is full of those who need the gifts only we, only you, only this parish, only those who hold the faith of Jesus can offer. God give us the joy and the strength to offer them all year long so that all God's wandering children one day can sing with us, Joy to the world! The Lord is come! Let earth receive her king!

Amen.

Patsy Davis' family has been in Mexico for generations.

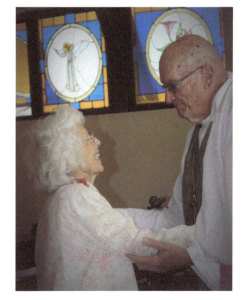

03 January 2016

The Second Sunday after Christmas

Jeremiah 31:7-14 Psalm 147:12-20 Ephesians 1:3-14 John 1:1-18

I reckon if I asked you, everybody here this morning could tell me what theology is, right? I won't call on you, don't worry, but it's a word we hear a good bit, especially in churches, and this morning, thanks to the gospel lesson you just heard, it's what we've got to deal with. Theology, if you pull the word apart into its two halves, means words about God. Simple as that, words about God. Any time we try to put our experience of God into words—and we don't always, often can't—we are doing theology. Some of you talk about your experience of God, at least you have with me, and so you are theologians when you do that. Ever think of yourself as a theologian? Well, when you try to talk about God, you are one, so there! Of course, there's theology and there's, ahem, Theology, once called "the divine science," what happens when religion goes to school and gets taken up by people who've read lots of books and know stuff and talk about God in ways you likely never would. The discipline has its own vocabulary, several of them in fact, and it should not be surprising that the dedicated study of the nature and behavior of God would keep a feller busy for a long time, trying to get all that figured out. Christianity has no monopoly on it, to be sure. As long as humans have been aware of God and wondering about God, they've done theology, and the books would fill a good many buildings bigger than this one. But we are a Christian congregation, and today's gospel lesson is probably, for Christian theologians anyway, the most important passage in the whole Bible. Its splendid, cascading language is the Bible's most far-reaching attempt to put the experience of Christ in Jesus into words, and in some ways the whole New Testament revolves around it and the splendid yet not simple message it conveys. (Fact is, back in the Middle Ages when the Roman Church was trying to convert the heathen up in Germany and Scandinavia, the pope fixed things so that passage was read at the end of every Mass, the priest standing at the north end of the altar and looking north, just to make sure the Huns heard it! Called it "the last gospel" and kept right on doing it long after Europe was converted, right on up to about 1970 or so. Habits hang on.) Ordinarily I don't like theological sermons and try not to preach them, the kind, I mean, where the preacher goes on telling about the tenses of Greek verbs and the arrangement of the Hebrew alphabet and all about the relationship between this or that article of the Nicene Creed. You may like that, and if you do, God bless you for it. I find it makes people look at their watches a good bit, and I can't blame them. But today we're up against it, so let me see how quick I can take care of what seems required to me—and it won't be real quick—and then see if I can hook the experience up to your life and mine in the Lord. Fasten your seat belts.

To put it as briefly as I can, this passage from John is the evangelist's attempt to put his experience and the infant church's experience of Jesus into words that encompass the big surprise Jesus was for a bunch of Jews waiting for a messiah of a certain kind and getting instead something far greater than and rather unlike what they expected. To do that, John had to step away from the old vocabulary of his Jewish-Hebrew upbringing and adapt some of the language of the Greek philosophical thought popular in his day, all the while staying smack in the heart of the Jewish experience of God. It is an amazing accomplishment. Jesus, remember, did not fit the job description of a Jewish messiah worth a dang, yet John affirms that he is the messiah. John, like Peter and many before him, senses that Jesus is not just a great teacher and healer but in fact is divine, is . . . well . . . God. How can that be? To the Jews, that was blasphemy, cut and dried, and we know their reaction to the claim. To say how that can be, John goes back to the beginning, to God himself, to God before the Big Bang, to God before anything we know ever started to be, back to the very nature of God; and he says, God is not quite so simple as we believed. The Jews affirm that God is One. John says that God is more than One, that God is a kind of community of One, and that is a paradox. To get at it, he takes a Greek word, *logos,* which means word, yes, but also means that which makes things understandable (whence our words logic, logical, and so on), and says that when God is God all by himself, God is both the almighty creator from whom all things come and at the same time is the Word, that which makes it possible for the creation, notably us human beings, to sense God, to hear God, to experience God intimately, in our own being. That Word, John says, was with God and was God before anything was created, and once creation happened, the Word was with God all through human history, man's long yearning and learning about God, principally the Jewish experience in this case. We heard hints of God's multiple personality in the lesson from Wisdom, all that about Wisdom dwelling with God from the beginning, not wisdom just as knowledge but rather as a kind of person; and the lesson from Ephesians claims that in Christ Jesus God has done what he purposed from before time began, to create a holy people to worship him and be his particular inheritance. Finally, John says, that Word became flesh, our flesh because he is talking about Jesus, and lived with us as one of us, and he is our messiah in ways the Jews never anticipated. What John is trying to articulate is what we call the mystery of the incarnation, of God taking flesh, and since *christos* is the Greek word that best translates the Hebrew for messiah, Jesus Christ is the messiah, the man who is also God and in whose life, death, and resurrection the body of Christ now lives. Whew. That is a mouthful, and I reckon I could gnaw around on it until the cows come home and not too many people would come down and surrender for missions to the Congo. But that's what theology does. It struggles to put words together to understand our experience of God, and thank God for it, even if it does seem awfully . . . abstract.

Now. I think it's important for me to lay all this before you on this rare occasion—we don't always get a Second Sunday after Christmas, depending on what day of the week Christmas comes on—because if nothing else it brings us face to face with the realization that what we are doing here is more than just gathering a bunch of people with a good bit in common to go through a drill we all know, dress it up with nice music and lots of fellowship and good feeling. A lot more than that. We are here because, understand it or not, we are holy beings caught up in the eternal divine drama, whatever that turns out to be. We have some notions, you bet, but just a whole lot of the time we are babes in arms, people who walk in darkness, and we come here to find light, divine light and guidance, divine communion in Jesus, divine sustenance at the Lord's table, divine mission in the teachings of our Blessed Lord. So I want to try to get hold of that mighty passage from John and see what people who are not theologians of the fancy kind can take home to live with.

Here goes. Notice the things that passage presumes. It presumes that we believe in God, first. It presumes that we believe God is good, not some scary, angry critter we need to hide from. It presumes that we believe that God is willing for us to know him; it presumes indeed that God knows we have a hard time and that he wants to help us, to care for us, to protect us. It presumes that God cares so much about us and our history that he has at least this once actually entered our history, that the Word who is God took our flesh and lived with us, that the *logos* came to make God understandable, reachable, knowable with an intimacy that is both outrageous and transforming. God the Christ became man in the Babe of Bethlehem, and from the man that baby became, we have received grace upon grace. Though none of us has ever seen God, nevertheless Jesus the Son of God who is close to God's own heart, who *is* God's heart, Jesus has made God known. That, I submit, is not abstract. It's about as real and fleshly as things can get, and that claim has caused people to ponder ever since John made it. Not everybody believes it by any means; a lot of Christians or people who think of themselves as Christians have a lot of trouble understanding it. It's not everyday, after all; it's a paradox and a mystery that none of us can ever wrap enough words around, because in the incarnation of Christ in Jesus, God has wrapped the eternal Word all around us. And how that works, well, each of us knows in ways that are often too deep for words.

Let me try to wrap this up by pointing to something somebody else noted about this passage recently. I speak of Her Majesty Queen Elizabeth II, that laywoman who is the titular head of this church to which we come to find Jesus. In her Christmas message this year, the Defender of the Faith recalled John's gentle reassurance that, though we deal with a lot of darkness in our lives day by day—in our individual lives, in our lives in the church, in our national and community lives—though we deal with a lot of darkness, John reminds us that the light of Christ still shines, that the darkness has not overcome it. That is reassurance I can cling to, by golly. I know that I live with plenty of darkness, both in myself and from without, but I also know that I have light, not only from my own heart but also from what we're doing right now. I know that all of you, one way or another, have to deal with darkness in your own lives. I know that people who never heard of Christ and millions who've heard of him but do not know him deal with darkness, a lot of darkness. At times, you can't blame people for growing despondent, for believing that God is either a fantasy or doesn't give a hoot about humanity or is just a cruel butcher. But amid all that circumstantial darkness, the light still rises. Christians still proclaim their faith and act on it. All around the world, Christian congregations, large and small, gather and pray and feed on Christ and go out to light candles in the darkness. I think that is proof of the truth in John's vision. The light still shines, all round the world. And at a more personal level, that this bunch of highly individual people who've come here from the four corners of the globe, this Christian congregation, gets itself out of bed on Sunday morning and puts on its make-up and grabs up a bag of beans to share with the hungry and comes in here and goes through a routine we all know and says Amen to prayers and shares God's peace at God's table, that is proof positive to me, at least, that the light of Christ shines on, that the darkness has not overcome it and, God willing, never will. And I think God is willing, willing that his light should shine in us and that we might live now and forever, knowing grace upon grace, blessing upon blessing, as God fulfills in us his loving purpose from all eternity. My cup runneth over.

Amen.

The parish once owned a spacious rectory which served as a kind of social center; but circumstances eventually required its sale. The first few times I visited, I stayed in the homes of parishioners or other clergy. In 2015, the vestry approved a single floor apartment in the garden behind the church. I lived in that when these sermons were preached. Subsequently they have added a second floor, creating a thoroughly inviting dwelling for clergy.

Directly opposite this little parsonage is the city's only English language library for which Saint Michael's provides space. It is in many ways the city's ex-pat social center. Dozens gather every Tuesday morning for tea or coffee and pastry, just to visit, catch up with one another, hear news and gossip. Most are not members of the parish but are often involved in parish events and outreach programs. A volunteer choir, the *Coro Deo Gracias,* led by the parish's music director, often rehearses in the building, providing lovely background music for evening reading.

Valedictory Comments and a Prone

10 January 2016

The First Sunday after Epiphany ~ The Feast of the Baptism of Christ

Isaiah 43:1-7 Psalm 29 Acts 8:14-17 Luke 3:15-17, 21-22

There's enough matter in those lessons we just heard for about four seventy-five dollar sermons in a row, but have no fear, I'm not going to do that. I've been here three months now, and you've heard me preach enough to know what my message is all about; and since this is my last Sunday with you for the near future, instead of preaching I want to spend a little time talking with you about my experience here with you, what I think I've learned, what I think we've accomplished together, and my take on the shape of the future for St. Michael's in the near term, plus a few observations—and maybe a little preaching after that. Carl here has already had a message this morning, someone afraid I was going to announce that the parish is being closed! Well, I'm sure not here to do that, not by a long shot.

Let me share with you how I came down here in the first place. As most of you know I've been coming to Cuernavaca since the 80s, when all this around here was countryside, Rio Mayo was just *empedrada*, and livestock grazed on the property. I first came to work with St. Michael's about ten years ago after Fr. Derby resigned, when the congregation was pretty small. On any Sunday morning I would find Patsy Davis and Nancy Blackmore and Ruth Winn here on the front pew, some other regulars scattered around, Andrea and the choir up in the loft. Twenty was a big crowd. I came back a year or so later, things not much changed. Then along about that time I learned that St. Michael's had up and elected a dadgummed ol' woman priest, Tamara Newell sitting right there, and what happened? Well, she absolutely transformed the place, that's what happened. I came back after she'd been here a couple of years, and the place was lip full, families with children, women having babies—well, not here in the church, but carrying them, you know what I mean!—Sunday school in operation, everybody chattering about taking food to the needy or carrying children to some museum, all about Christian ministry outside the doors. It was just amazing. Lila Solt handed me a book on emerging church principles that helped me understand what was going on. But then as happens, circumstances changed. The mining industry in Morelos collapsed, lots of those families moved away. There were some important funerals. With the bad press Mexico has these days, thanks in part to people like Donald Trump, not many new gringos are arriving to fill in the gaps. Tamara decided to retire and enjoy life with her family, as was perfectly proper. One thing and another. Then one day last September, I got a message from your friend Steven Spencer saying, "There are problems at St. Michael's. Can you come for six months?" I answered that at my time of life I almost never commit to anything that far down the line, but I figured I might come for three. When I came I thought I was coming to pick up the pieces and get the parish ready to call its next rector. I knew pretty soon and am now entirely convinced, that's not going to happen for some time. There's just not the human capital here to do that, so for the near future your vestry is going to advertise St. Michael's as a chaplaincy, so to speak, invite people like me, retired, likely unmarried, to come and stay with you from two to three months to provide Sunday services and other pastoral oversight as needed in return for what is in effect an all expenses paid vacation in this lovely city. (I say unmarried, by the way, because that nifty little bungalow I'm in is right . . . snug. A married couple living there would have to be mighty tolerant of each other to survive!) We have already circularized the job announcement in about nine dioceses that border Mexico, as well as Los Angeles. I must say, some of the responses I've had from deployment officers in those dioceses were discouraging, something like, "Well now, isn't that interesting. I can't think of anybody right now, but if I do, I'll let you know." Duh. My thought is, "Could ya just publish it?" For Pete's sake! But when I get home, I've got some ideas how we might do better. In the meantime, if you know people who fit that description, let your vestry know, okay? I have tentatively committed to coming back a couple of months this summer, when Texas is unbearable, especially if my children will come visit then, too. But in the near future, that's about what the situation is in brief.

That said, I'd like to review some of the things I think we've accomplished since I got here. A question I asked a lot was, "What's broken at St. Michael's? What can we fix now?" Believe me, I got lots of feedback.

- Let me start with a notable exception. Everybody assured me that one thing was not broken, namely the music. The music doesn't need fixing. Andrea and the choir have not shown a feather, and that needs no fixing. And, of course, they were right. Thank God for that.

- Now, if you go inside that door up there beside the altar, that's where the sacristies are. A sacristy is the place where all the vestments and the holy doodads we use in worship are kept and made ready for worship every Sunday. Let me tell you, the first time I walked in there, I was pretty upset. They were chaotic, jammed full of things that had no business in there, kind of scary. I told Sandy, any priest considering coming here would take one look and be right out the door. Well, that was an easy fix really, just a lot of moving out and throwing away and cleaning up and organizing. I'm happy to say that today they are beautiful and spic and span, just as the kitchen that serves God's table should be. And I asked for some help from an altar guild, and some have stepped up, though more of you need to volunteer for that work.

- Another matter was St. Michael's relation to the bishop of the diocese. For a long list of reasons some of you know too well, this congregation's dealings with a succession of bishops have been somewhat strained and with considerable reason. I got here on a Thursday, and the next day I was over at the office to say *a sus órdenes* to Bishop Treviño. The whole experience was delightful. I believe you have at last a truly godly and quite humble pastor in him; and I am aware that at recent meetings between him and some of your vestry here, everything was sweetness and light. That's as it should be, because for better, for worse, St. Michael's is an Anglican church in union with the convention of the Diocese of Cuernavaca, and I hope the relation stays good going forward.

- Communications. I am so grateful to Kay Godfrey that she has resumed the weekly e-mail communication with the congregation and others. If you don't check your e-mail for that, please start. One of the biggest problems I found here was rumor, *chisme*, what St. Paul called "unprofitable conversation" about what was going on, what wasn't, who had the button. The simple fact is, if folks aren't given good information, they'll manufacture their own, and it's not always malicious, just sort of unavoidable. So I am really thankful that is back in operation. Please give it your support by reading it.

• I knew that the Spanish speaking congregation of San Pablo, whose building this was originally, worshipped here Sunday evenings, but I was pretty amazed to learn that relations with them had gone way sour. Every Sunday when we finished up, we had what I called *la guerra de los candados*. All the locks were changed, everything not heavy was moved back into the priest's sacristy, and all was locked and barred! I was told that was because "they would steal us blind." Well, I couldn't fathom that, so I took it on myself to meet their priest, Padre Chava—Father Salvador Martínez, dean at the cathedral downtown—and found him just a delightful man. Thank God, the lock swapping stopped, and as you know that congregation joined us for Christmas Eve Mass and Fr. Chava helped at the altar. I hope that rapprochement grows and that St. Michael's and San Pablo grow together more and more. Two Christian families sharing a house of worship should get along!

• I worked with Marisela Lathrop to take part in the Fall ingathering of the United Thank Offering of the women of the church at Alpuyeca, and I know a lot of you took home UTO Blue Boxes. I don't know how many of you are using them, but I hope you are. It's a good work.

• I learned soon that much of the bustling energy devoted to Christian outreach that so delighted me a few years back had sort of dried up and fallen almost wholly on the shoulders of this lady sitting at my left hand. You've heard me again and again on that topic, and while I know many of you are involved in lots and lots of good work on your own, I still think the congregation needs to practice outreach as a family. I'm proud of the way you responded to the needs of the orphanage in Monte Casino, and I am really proud of the way you've filled the food basket the last couple of Sundays. Please send me away with at least the delusion that bringing something for the food basket every Sunday is going to become part of you parish culture.

• Finally I believe that a lot of the sense of trust and affection and goodwill that had suffered recently has been regained, a lot of wounds beginning to heal. It's no secret that my predecessor was controversial, and I have heard a lot from a lot of you. I can tell you that there are people here who will defend Fr. Bufkin right down the line; and there are others whose feelings are rather different. I know that he has caused me not a single problem since I have been here, and as I published a while ago, the bishop is working with him to determine his future. The proper thing for everyone here is to pray for him and for the bishop that they might discern the best course of action for his good and the good of the Church. Beyond that, I welcome the atmosphere of trust and affection that you have offered me.

Let me turn now to some observations, not judgments, not instructions precisely, since that's not my function, but some thoughts I'd like to offer for your consideration going forward.

- First, the somewhat unique character of this congregation. Since St. Michael's is the only English speaking congregation in Cuernavaca, we gladly welcome a good many people from other Christian traditions, and that's wonderful. Misunderstandings can arise, however, about how decisions are reached. What may not be clear to some is how an Anglican congregation is governed, how it makes decisions. Our church has a centuries old tradition of how authority operates under the leadership of diocesan bishops, and it is not exactly democratic. The congregation as a whole makes only two decisions at the annual parish meeting: it elects vestry people and it approves a budget. Beyond that decisions are made by the vestry according to very carefully defined canon laws. I am aware that some people here do not entirely understand that—and, I hasten to add, through no fault of their own. I am recommending to the vestry in a separate report that they strive to keep the congregation informed when decisions affecting everyone are made. Since we are not many, misunderstanding often gets personalized, and we must work very diligently to help each other understand the context.
- The matter usually called stewardship needs attention. Many have told me you are reluctant to sign a pledge card because you really don't know where the money is going, and I understand that. It is, however, just about impossible for your vestry to budget for ministry when they have no idea what resources will be at their disposal at any given moment. About the best they can do is report an expense budget. I am encouraging them to communicate with you regularly about income and outgo and about planning going forward. I want to encourage all of you to consider making an annual pledge for the good of St. Michael's and the wider Church. I lay it to your conscience.
- I cannot stress enough the importance of good communication within the congregation. Please support Kay's efforts and find ways to increase the flow of good information among yourselves. Above all, fend off the temptation to take sides and find fault. Let all your conversation be positive and in a spirit of brotherly and sisterly love. Let those superb admonitions from Ephesians we heard a couple of weeks ago be your guide.
- Finally, turn your eyes outward. Concentrate on how St. Michael's can share the wealth it has, and I'm not talking about money. You come here because you find something here. Well, share that with your friends who don't go to church anywhere. Talk St. Michael's up. Lord, the crowd that gathers at the library for tea every Tuesday, the many social gatherings you go to, those are fields white to the harvest. Commend St. Michael's to them when you can.

Well. You notice I didn't invoke the Holy Trinity when I started this, but now perhaps I will. In the name of God, Amen. I want now to share with you my vision of what the mission of St. Michael's is for the near future. This is the Feast of the Baptism of Christ, when Jesus submitted to the baptism of John as a sign of the free forgiveness of sin and God's acceptance of Jesus and of you and of me as his beloved children. Many of you have told me that you treasure the community and the fellowship you find here, and I have no argument with that. I cannot say too often, however, that there is something more than that going on here. This is a congregation of people baptized into the death and resurrection of Christ Jesus, people who at one time or another committed themselves as Christ's faithful followers unto their lives' end. This is not just a society of like minded people. We are involved in the eternal struggle between good and evil, between light and darkness, between life and death, and when we gather here we are a holy people, raised to heavenly realms and replenished for lives of grace and goodness. St. Michael's is here for a reason. You know I don't like to talk about God having plans. How many planning meetings have you been to? Weren't they fun? And how soon after the plan went into action did you have to change it? We don't do God any favors when we call him a planner. But I do believe that God has *purposes*, and purposes endure. St. Michael's is here as part of God's eternal purpose of incarnating his overflowing, self-effacing, self-sacrificing love in your flesh and mine, so we can bear that light to those who know it not. Right now just to maintain that witness may be about all St. Michaels' can manage, but if that's so, don't fret about it. Embrace it. Lift your heads and your spirits and smile and step right up to the job. And be on the watch for change, because change comes, often when we least expect it, when suddenly the Holy Spirit provides new opportunities. Above all, be joyful and grateful and generous, always trusting in God's goodness and Jesus' love and the Holy Spirit's leading.

Thank you again for inviting me to work with you. The last words I want to say to you come from St. Luke's gospel: Fear not, little flock. It is God's good pleasure to give you the Kingdom.

Amen.

No wall in Mexico is safe from muralists . . . including graffiti artists. This wall encloses the garden of a school on upper Humboldt Avenue. The thought balloon's message: "A day without creating is a day lost." Ya reckon?

The imposing west doors of the former convent church of Dominico de la Natividad, a World Heritage Site in Tepoztlán, about a half hour's drive up into the mountains from Cuernavaca. Built by forced labor between 1555 and 1580, the building is still a parish church with an active worshiping community. Next to it is the punctiliously restored convent, a museum open to the public. Stenciled frescoes adorn the walls and ceilings, scds of angels and cherubs each with a slightly different face. The monks' cells, an infirmary, a library, an impressive refectory, and carefully symmetrical interior gardens make a slow visit worthwhile. Most amusing are the mildly obscene instructions on proper defecation on the walls above the latrines. The museum often hosts exhibitions of local artists' work.

The city of Tepoztlán (about 40,000 inhabitants, swelled on weekends by droves of rowdy visitors) is one of Mexico's *pueblos mágicos* where colonial architecture predominates and to which pre-Columbian cultures attached spiritual significance. Myth has it that the town is the birthplace of Quetzalcoatl, the feathered serpent god.

12 June 2016

Fourth Sunday after Pentecost

1 Kings 21:1-21a Psalm 5:1-8 Galatians 2:15-21 Luke 7:36-8:3

Before I get to the sermon, let me say what a joy it is to be back among you here at St. Michael's after half a year's sojourn at home in Texas. After I got here Thursday afternoon, Carl Haymes took me to supper, and after we ate he asked, "How does it feel to be back?" I thought a minute and said, "It feels comfortable." And it does, really comfortable and reassuring to be back in this wonderful place here with you in God's house. Thank you for asking me to come back.

As you see, I come to you in the long green season, and thank God these vestments are a little lighter than those I wore in the winter. As you will recall, in the Pentecost season we take up one of the gospels—Luke this year—and work our way through it Sunday by Sunday. Along with that we follow some of the great narrative strands of the Old Testament—the Book of Kings just now—plus a psalm, and we read from the New Testament epistles, right now Paul's to the Galatians. My job, our job, is to consider those lessons and see what the Holy Spirit is trying to say to the church this morning, then incorporate what we learn into the way we lead our lives day by day. And as you may recall, I often like to start our journey through the lessons by reviewing the collect for the day, to which you just said Amen. Or at least some of you did!

The Prayer Book collects have a fairly consistent form. We address God—God, Almighty God, Father in Heaven, Lord—and then we attribute something to God, often some gift bestowed on us; after that we ask for grace to do something specific in response to the gift. Today's collect is exactly in that form. We affirm that God keeps his household in steadfast faith and love. That has implications. First, we claim our place in God's household, claim that we are God's children, the apples of the divine eye. That claim entails our obligation to behave like God's children and is fodder for lots of sermons. But there's more. We claim that by grace we have faith, that our hearts and minds shape our lives according to God's teaching. We also claim that we live in the power and under the protection of God's never-failing, all-forgiving love. Already we've said a good many mouths full. But there's more. We ask that, given the foregoing, we be able to proclaim God's truth with boldness, and that request implies that we will encounter some things, some experiences contrary to God's truth, some lie, some untruth that deforms divine reality (which we are learning to recognize) and that when we meet that untruth we oppose it with God's truth. That's a job that will get you in trouble. And if we prevail and see truth overcome untruth, we are not to gloat and recriminate; rather we are to "administer" God's justice with compassion. It always shocks us when we remember that justice is a human concept, a moralizing system through which we try to achieve a kind of balance between good and bad behavior—and it usually involves punishment and far too often induces a sense of our own superiority. God, however, is not just; God is merciful, and divine mercy wipes away guilt and renews the bond of love. This could go on and on, the implications flying in all directions, but I think we've got plenty of framework already to get to the lessons.

Today we've got two great stories plus a psalm and Paul in a pique. The first great story is part of a long narrative of the kings of Israel and Judah, most of them bad guys, and the prophets who boldly proclaimed God's truth in the face of their manifold untruths. Today we pick up where we left off with the story of Elijah's ongoing battle with Ahab, the baddest of the bad. You remember a couple of Sundays ago we saw Elijah facing down 450 Baal prophets, chopping up all kinds of livestock and calling down fire from Heaven. Today's episode is not quite so bloody, but it's still plenty interesting. Evidently a fellow named Naboth owned a vineyard near some property of Ahab's, and Ahab wanted it to plant a vegetable garden, a likely story. He goes to Naboth and asks me for it, says he'll give him money and another piece of property better yet. Naboth turns him down flat, says he couldn't think of selling his inheritance, no, not doing it. Ahab stomps off back to the palace where he pulls an epic pout, falls into bed, turns his face to wall and whines, "Bad ol' Naboth won't give me his vineyard, and I am so mad I'm going to puff up like a pouter pigeon and hold my breath till I turn blue and I'm not even going to eat my supper, so there!" Enter Queen Jezebel. Wow. What a gal. Since I've been here I watched a recent Scottish re-make of Macbeth on Netflix, all grim and rainy and cold and spooky, probably would suit Shakespeare—though the Scots brogue made it all but incomprehensible to me, and I know the play by heart. Anyway that brought on Lady Macbeth, one of the Bard's most astonishing characters, and as I watched her tongue lash her hesitant husband, I wondered if Shakespeare had Jezebel in mind when he created Mrs. Macbeth. Jezebel asks Ahab what's eating him, he tells her, and she says, "Lord, you are such a ninny! Are you king here or not? Get up and get in there and eat your supper and by the time you're done, I'll give you Naboth's vineyard myself. Jerk!" And he does and she does, frames Naboth, gets him killed, comes back with the deed to the property, and nearly gets by with it. Except for Elijah. God sends him to Ahab to ask him if he indeed killed Naboth and stole his vineyard, "killed and taken possession." What the lesson does not tell you is that Jewish law prohibited people from selling off inherited land, a kind of estate entailment system that kept family property together from generation to generation, so Ahab's demand meant forcing Naboth to sin and Jezebel doubled down on that by murdering him. "Have you found me, my enemy? Yes, I did," Ahab retorts. "So what?" And Elijah tells him what. He has sinned twice and will be brought to destruction. The lesson today stops there and might leave us with a sense of considerable satisfaction that justice had been done. But if we read on just a little, we learn that God decided to let Ahab live some longer, which is a way of saying that he, not Elijah, would decide what happened to Ahab. See how that parallels the collect? Elijah boldly proclaimed God's truth and added a dire threat of condign punishment; but God reserved to himself how that justice would work out.

Now Paul and the Galatians. I have to say, the letter to the Galatians is not Paul at his best. He started a congregation in Galatia, probably part Jews, part Gentiles, and gave them the gospel of love to replace the old religion of rules and works. In today's lesson we hear him reiterating the priority of faith and love over that old guilt management system, and the collect speaks to that in a way. But let me remind you that Paul was as mad as an old wet hen. The letter starts of with a florid greeting, telling them how proud of them he is, how their faith is a shining example, how he prays for them and loves them. New paragraph. "You stupid Galatians!" I quote. And then he just takes the hide off their backs because they had listened to people who told them that, no no, they had to keep the old Jewish laws. I reckon we can give the second lesson a nod today and get on to the gospel.

Oh Luke. I'm so glad we're doing Luke this year, because he is one of the great story-tellers of all time, which sure pleases the English teacher in me, and today's story is among his most memorable. Jesus has been out in public long enough to make a name for himself, pretty off-the-blanket a lot of the time but doing amazing things and gathering a following. A Pharisee invites him to eat at his house. Now remember, the Pharisees come in for a lot of bad press in the gospels, but in their day they were the good guys. They kept the law scrupulously, they paid tithes, they prayed up a storm in public. They were the leaders in the Jewish church, at least the vestry, maybe the executive council, and for a Pharisee to invite somebody like Jesus to lunch took . . . well . . . he probably felt he was really being big about things, having this street preacher into his house. So Jesus joins the party, though he's not invited to the head table, just goes in and sits among the other guests. Before long a "woman of the city, a sinner" slips in carrying a jar of expensive ointment, kneels at Jesus' feet, anoints him, kisses his feet, and washes them with her tears. Now this woman is often identified with Mary Magdalene, and when the text says "sinner" we know for sure she's a streetwalker. The Pharisee sees that and . . . well, what would you think if that happened at some party you gave? He takes it in and all his moral superiority kicks in. "Look at that! What kind of a preacher is he if he doesn't know that woman is a you-know-what. Disgusting hussy, carrying on like that. Harrumph!" Certainly he regrets asking that kind of trash into his house. Notice now that the gospel does not say he said that out loud, though he may have. In any case, Jesus can see the sanctimonious body language and calls him out—boldly proclaims God's truth in the face of hypocrisy—"Simon, I've got something to say to you." Follows the parable of the two debtors and the question, "Who loved most?" The Pharisee knows he's cornered and gives the obvious answer: "The one who was forgiven most." Then Jesus runs the bill of particulars: you didn't give me water to wash my feet, but this woman washed them with her tears; you didn't greet me with a kiss, but this woman is kissing my feet; you didn't anoint my head, but this woman has anointed my feet." We don't know his tone of voice, but the sarcasm is thick. What the text doesn't report but surely Jesus thought was, "And Simon, you don't know the first thing about love." Well now. Talk about proclaiming God's truth boldly! And then he turns to the woman, whose sins he acknowledges, they are many, and tells her she's forgiven. Wow. That probably blew the Pharisee right out of his chair, and all the people watching dumbstruck begin to ask themselves, "Who is this guy?" He "administered justice" not with vengeance but with compassion, forgiveness. Love.

When we turn from the scripture and look at our lives, I think we can see ourselves all over these lessons and in that collect. We who are indeed God's household, we run into plenty of sin and lies and other distortions of God's purpose in our lives day by day. Lord God, just watch the news if you've got any doubt. The question the collect poses is, what do we do about that? Way too often we run hide in a corner and say, "Oh, I'm just one person and I can't get involved in all that." But we said Amen to a prayer that impels us to proclaim God's truth boldly, and by golly, sometimes we manage to do it. In our public life, look at what's been going on in this city, protests in the streets almost every day from people who aren't getting what they think they've earned. Yeah, it botches up traffic something awful and irritates us if we're trying to cross the city; but those people are standing up against a perceived evil and are willing to take the consequences. In our lives, public and private, we have to learn to do the same, though maybe with less disruption. As citizens we should not condone chicanery, but rather we should try to be good citizens ourselves and lead by example. In the church too. When somebody in a congregation thinks there's a flaw, to say nothing is to condone it, and we can always come to each other in love and try to work things out for the good of the whole family. Don't sull up like Ahab. And in our own private lives, this day teaches us not to ignore the sins in our self or in others but rather to face them and pray for grace to overcome them in ourselves and to love others toward better health. Above all it teaches us not to strut and gloat and, like Shylock, insist on the last pound of flesh, the last drop of blood, but rather to forgive as we are forgiven and go the extra mile for reconciliation.

One more story and we're done. My son Stephen is a lot like me, positive he's right because he thinks things through. Recently he encountered a situation he considered untruth. His youngest, Molly Kay, my youngest grandchild, is a smart little girl in third grade, plenty bright; but she inherited the family number defect and is having trouble with math. He and his wife got tutors, helped Molly with math enhancement programs online and elsewhere, finally decided they needed to turn to the school system. Took Molly Kay to be tested by the special education team in the public school she attends, got back an answer that she didn't qualify for special programs, might need a tutor or some enhancement programs. That answer wouldn't do, looked flat wrong, not true. So he turned to his elder sister, an expert in special education, currently principal of the special education high school in a Texas school district. She asked for a telephone conference with the special ed people at Molly's school, reviewed the tests with them, showed them that oh yeah oh yeah she qualified for special programs, no doubt about it. The meeting ended without a decision, and Stephen told me he figured they wouldn't accept her, was ready to apply the grievance procedures. But know what? Lo and behold, couple days later they called and said, Okay, she qualifies. Of course he felt justified and with every right; but my fatherly counsel was that when the work began he be as conciliatory and cooperative and appreciative as possible. I believe he will, because he's also smart like me!

Here's the take home. The world is full of untruth and distortion. We meet it day by day. We are God's children, protected but also empowered and commanded to face it boldly with God's truth. We are not always going to win, but when we do we must not then become oppressors ourselves. Rather we are to work with those who don't know God the way we do, to bring them to God by example and loving act. It's a full-time job and not always fun, but those are the marching orders we all said Amen to just now.

Amen.

19 June 2016

Fifth Sunday after Pentecost

1 Kings 19:1-15a Psalm 42 and 43 Galatians 3:23-29 Luke 8:26-39

Wasn't that some prayer we said Amen to just now as the Eucharist opened? Today's collect departs from the usual format a little. Instead of addressing God and making some claim about Him, we go straight to asking for a gift—and what a gift that is! We ask for a "perpetual love and reverence" for God's name. That word perpetual, now, that means never failing, never flagging, never in doubt, absolutely rock solid. Remember that. Then comes the matter of what we are to love and revere, God's "holy Name." Technically that's Yahweh, Jehovah in lots of translations, and to the Hebrews it was so sacred they couldn't even say it, and to some degree they used it almost as a conjure word, a talisman. We don't think of it that way, and I'd say what we mean with this prayer is that we love and revere all we know of God, God's love, God's purpose with us. And finally we identify ourselves as those set upon the sure foundation of God's lovingkindness, God's household, God's chillen. Amen and amen.

Now that's a big prayer, just about says it all, doesn't it? That's the whole gospel in one sentence right there, and we could just close up shop and go on to lunch . . . except. Except for life. When I was a kid I was fascinated with the history of World War II, which I remembered only vaguely because it was over when I was four, but I remembered it; and that's what everybody talked about for the next ten years at least. I had a couple of old vinyl 33rpm records, Columbia Records, called *I Can Hear It Now*, narrated by Edward R. Murrow, clips from radio news broadcasts, and one that sticks in memory and came to me as I pondered what to say today was Stalin. Pardon me for mentioning his name, but when I was a kid, he was still alive and we were scared silly of him. I remember his voice, monotonous and indistinct and in Russian of course, but it was a May Day speech from about 1943 during the siege of Leningrad, and the translation was, "I speak to you today in difficult times." Difficult times. Man, that's a pregnant phrase. That was war time, of course, but ya know? When are times not difficult? Life gives us breathers now and then, but as far as I know, times are difficult right on down the line. Lord, if you doubt that, turn on the news. The horror in Orlando last week and plenty more convince me, we are living in difficult times, certainly in our public lives but often enough in our more private lives, in our families, among our friends, in church, with our own souls. Plenty of difficult times. And what is the question we invariably hear after something like Orlando? You know it: "Where is God in all this? How can God let things like this happen? Where is now your God?" to quote today's psalm. Well I gotta tellya, I think that's the wrong question, and when I hear that my response is, "Right where he's always been. The question is, where are *we*? What's got hold of us that we let things like that happen?" You may remember the war for the Falklands. Argentina decided they wanted the Malvinas back and invaded; Maggie Thatcher sent the British fleet, the consummate act of empire. When it was all over, I remember some leader in Argentina asking, *"Qué tenemos nosotros argentinos?* What's wrong with us Argentines?" That was the right question to ask, and the Brits might have asked it as well. The point is that in difficult times we are prone to feel like the sure foundation of God's lovingkindness has shattered, and our perpetual love and reverence is severely challenged. I and a lot of people I've met in the last half century have had that experience, some are living with it right now, so I think the question is, When we get into that pickle, how do we get back onto solid footing with our faith in God? For some help, let's have a look at today's amazing lessons.

We've got Elijah again this morning, and Jezebel is on his case. Ahab as usual whines to her about Elijah killing 450 Baal prophets a couple of weeks ago, and her response is no surprise: "So help me Baal, you go tell Elijah I'm gonna do that and worse to him by this time tomorrow!" Elijah hears that, and he is afraid—with reason. I mean, he's got the Old Testament Lady Macbeth after him, so he hies out into the desert to hide and talk to God about it. "God, I've had enough! Enough! Just kill me now. I have had it." I can't read that without recalling Mendelssohn's wonderful oratorio *Elijah* and a magnificent baritone aria on those words: It is enough! Well now. Have you ever felt that way? Sure you have. I know I have, more than once. For one reason or another, life gets so wadded up and twisted and contorted and ungodly, maybe our own fault, maybe not, but you finally get to the point where you just want to crawl in a hole and pull it in after you. Enough! Kill me or let me alone but enough! What the lectionary doesn't include is that an angel came from God and fixed him a little loaf of bread and sent him to Mount Horeb where he meets God who asks him, "What are you doing here?" Elijah repeats his complaint, so God puts on a show. A great wind rips the place apart, but God is not there. Then an earthquake, but God is not there. Then a fire, ditto. And finally silence and out of that silence, God asks again, "What are you doing here? Get up and get back on the road. Into the wilderness." Hmm. Not very comforting, that. When we're whipped into wanting to quit and surrounded by the silence of God, the message is, "What are you doing out here? Hitch up your britches and get back on the road." Yet as it turns out, that's the way God's love revives us and restores us to the sure foundation of his lovingkindness. Talk about tough love! The lesson is that even in Elijah's exhaustion and discouragement, God does not abandon him. He's not in the racket and the hooraw and the storm and earthquake and fire of our lives but rather in that still, small voice that speaks to a frightened child. Go on now, you'll be okay. I'm with you.

We get much the same in the psalm, don't we? "As a deer longs for flowing streams, so my soul longs for you, O God." An old hymn based on Psalm 42 rather neatly upped the ante on the sense of longing: "As pants the hart for cooling streams / When heated in the chase." In the chase invokes the image of a deer hunt, when the dogs of life are after you and closing in. I come from deer hunting country. My mother's home was McCulloch County, population about 8,500 people and 40,000 thousand or so deer the last time they flew over and tried to count. I'm not a hunter. I couldn't shoot Bambi's mother, but my father was, my son is, my son-in-law is, two of my grandchildren are. Believe me, the way people hunt deer today—just a quick shot to kill—is far more humane than the way they hunted them when that hymn was written three centuries ago, setting the hounds on them, the poor things crashing headlong through the forests, hearing the baying dogs and smelling death. Lord, what torture! That really intensifies the metaphor, doesn't it? But just like

Elijah in the wilderness, that psalm turns a corner and asks the right questions. As people sneer—Where is your God?—the singer asks his soul, "What are you doing here? Hope in God and praise him." You see how the pattern repeats? When your heart is bursting with anxiety and fear and a sense of abandonment, sing God's praises, because he is your strong defender. There's that sure foundation of lovingkindness again, isn't it? Yet we know that sense of fear and loss and abandonment, and at times it's pretty hard to remember the way out.

Let's turn to the gospel now, another wonderful acted parable from Luke and one of the most puzzling—and amusing—stories in the New Testament. I mean, look at it. Jesus has wandered off into Gentile territory, the Gerasene country where no good Jew has any business being. What he finds there is absolute disorder: a crazy man, demon possessed, running around naked in the cemetery causing such an uproar they have to chain him up; but he breaks the chains and runs around . . . a real mess. And the minute he sees Jesus, the demons know who he is and ask him to leave them alone. (Now . . . this is the Episcopal Church. The Episcopal Church doesn't do demons, does it? No, Episcopalians don't do demons. But yeah, the gospel does demons, Jesus does demons, so we need to do demons for a minute before we go on. I Googled demons up, and is there ever a lot of info there plus some really fabulous images. Since Christianity comes out of the Middle East, I checked out that bunch of demons, usually called djinns, where we get the word genie. You know, a feller finds a lamp and rubs it and out comes a genie. They're connected with fire, they can be good or bad, and they're usually some kind of magic, can grant wishes or turn you into a loathsome toad. Most people don't believe that way nowadays, but if you do, that's your business. That doesn't mean demons don't exist. The way I think of them comes from the Greek word *daemon* and has been used by psychologists I've read to mean some part of a whole being that takes over and distorts and misdirects that whole, not some scary critter from without but something within that metastasizes and destroys the host, the way healthy patriotism in a nation can turn into chauvinism and imperialism and wreak havoc. Now I know those exist. I speak from experience. A good many times in my life, some part of me, some aspect of my whole put-together, has taken charge and played Hell with my life. Sometimes with my cooperation, at others sort of sneaking up on me, but in every case sending my life careening down a bad road and hurting me and lots of other people around me until finally I woke up and wanted to crawl into that hole and pull it in after me. Then some angel has given me a little loaf of bread, often without me even knowing it when it happened, and set me on the road to sanity and health again. Those unruly parts are still with me, but they're no longer in control, and God grant they never are again. It is plenty scary and plenty real, and if you're anything like me, you've had the same experience. We've all got our demons.) Well, back to Jesus and the demoniac. He asks them their name, and the answer is Legion. A legion is, you know, six thousand Roman soldiers. "Legion. Many. Plenty. But please don't send us back where we can't have fun and raise Hell." So what does he do? Sends them into a herd of pigs that then charges down a hillside into the lake and drowns. I've always wanted to hear this sermon preached from the point of view of the poor swineherds! Naturally, the news gets around, and the people in the village come and find Jesus sitting and chatting with the man, sane as can be.

Scares them to death, and they beg Jesus to get out of town and leave them alone. When he agrees to go, the healed man begs to go with him, and as you heard, Jesus says essentially the same thing God said to Elijah, "Go back home and tell everybody what wonderful things God has done for you." Think of that.

Paul finally and quickly. He's at last found the happy message in the unhappy letter to the Galatians, and it is powerful. You used to be chained by laws you could not obey, must have felt like a deer in a hunt, must have wanted to say Enough! But now you are set free, clothed in Christ, and made one with him. And if you belong to Christ, you are heirs of the promise of God. There's that sure foundation of God's lovingkindness again. I don't think I have to elaborate.

Now. What's the take-home from all this? A good many things. One is that despite our faith in God's lovingkindness, from time to time we find ourselves living in difficult times, times that can shake us hard and make us feel like a deer with the dogs behind it. Another is that, far from abandoning us, God knows that and somehow some way sends angels to bake us a little cake, a little touch of Christ's healing love we may not recognize when it comes. Yet another is that when that love flowers and that restoration is fulfilled—it happens a thousand thousand ways, everyone's experience unique yet similar to others'—we are freed to sing God's praise again and to declare how much God has done for us. We who are set upon the foundation of God's lovingkindness forget our love and reverence for his Name, no matter the why; and then it's only God's amazing grace that seeks out lost sheep and carries them back home to safety. That is a scary story, but it has a wondrous ending.

So as we wind this up, let me say four things. First, if you've never had such an experience, be thankful but be aware it can happen. Second, if you've had the experience or a lot of it, God bless it to you. When I was in seminary fifty years ago I knew the Sisters of St. Anne in Chicago, and they said that a lot. Whatever you said, May God bless that to you. I never quite figured out the theological ins and outs of that, but I knew what they meant. God turns everything, good and bad, into blessing one way or another. Third, when you leave here remember that people all over the place are in the hands of their demons, some you know. If you run onto that, don't be afraid. You don't have to be pushy, but maybe you can just bake a little cake and leave it on a rock, some little touch of Jesus' love which may be what gives them the strength to turn again and finally one day find God again. Fourth, any time and any place, declare how much God has done for you. That's your theme for now and in Glory.

Amen.

The iconic view of the heart of the city from the balcony of Cortez' Palace, the oldest conserved colonial-era civil structure in America, north or south. The building began as a fortified residence for Hernán Cortés, built in 1526, over a Tlahuica Aztec tribute collection center the Spanish destroyed during the Conquest. During the Mexican War of Independence it held prisoners such as José María Morelos y Pavón, the revolutionary priest for whom the state is named. After the war, it became the seat of the state government until the late twentieth century, when the government moved and the structure was renovated and converted into the current Museo Regional Cuauhnahuac with exhibits on the history of Morelos. Calle Hidalgo runs from the Palace to the Cathedral, visible in the distance. If you look closely you can see crenellations for cannons above the dome. The central plaza or *zócalo*, under repair in 2016, is to the right.

Here you see Calle Hidalgo filled to the brim with that most Mexican of all social events, a march to protest something. Few days pass without such outbursts, brought on by first this, then the next outrage somebody has perpretrated on somebody else. People opposed to the state government's approval of same-sex marriage in Morelos organized this march in July 2016. Evidently a plebiscite showed only two of the state's municipalities—Cuernavaca and Tepoztlán—in favor, yet the legislature approved the law anyway. All the people in this march wore white T-shirts imprinted with their message. Who paid for them? When the marchers reached the Palace, they gathered round and sang and shouted in response to a man with a bullhorn. Not unlike a pep rally.

    The yellow building opposite is a popular restaurant, Casa Hidalgo. The church at upper left is not the cathedral but rather a shrine with an astonishing gilt reredos.

26 June 2016

Sixth Sunday after Pentecost

2 Kings 2:1-2, 6-14 Psalm 77:1-2, 11-20 Galatians 5:1, 13-25 Luke 9:51-62

This morning's collect is mighty specific, isn't it? As you know, our collects usually start with some rather abstract attributions to God, but not today. "You have built your Church upon the foundation of the apostles and prophets, Jesus Christ himself being the chief cornerstone." That is a statement of historical fact, nothing abstract about it, and it brings us face to face with handing the faith of Jesus along through the generations, as well as with the church fact we call the apostolic succession, something you should have learned about in confirmation class. For the preacher that's a temptation, namely, to avoid today's lessons and preach a didactic sermon, all full of good information and instruction; but I suspect that if I treated you to such a spectacle, you'd treat me to a lot of watch-checking and yawn-stifling and eyeball-rolling, so I'm not going to do that. I do, however, want to deal with that term, apostolic succession, quick quick. If you don't know, the theory is that since Jesus gave the keys of the kingdom to Peter and Peter was the first pope—theory, I said, theory—then Peter passes the keys along to the next pope, to Linus then Anacletus then Clement then Evaristus and right on down the line to blessèd Francis today, unbroken—of course, we Anglicans get a little hiccup with Henry VIII and all that, but it's pretty solid on down the line to the American Church and thence to the Mexican Church and our good Bishop Enrique next door—and that reassures us that the faith is maintained pure and undefiled. Yeah? Ri-i-ight. I and some others suspect they weren't keeping lists of popes back then, and even if they were when you consider some of the men who've occupied the throne of Peter, well. Lutherans and other Reformation churches lean rather more heavily on the succession of the magisterium of the faith *per se*, not so dependent on fallible men, while lots of churches sort of make it all up as they go along. And until the last century, women were just about not in the game at all. So. If all that is in question, what is sure? Well, look around you. We're here, and in thousands of buildings more or less like this one around the world, the Body of Christ is alive and relatively well and usually kicking about something. The Church, Jesus Christ himself being the chief cornerstone, is here, so there's no doubt the faith has been passed along. End of didactic sermon. On to the lessons, all of which illuminate that great collect.

From the Old Testament we've got the end of the Elijah story we've been following the past month or so. You'll remember last Sunday Elijah was ready to holler calf-rope, I've had enough, just kill me now, I quit. You remember too that God turned him right around and sent him back to work. But today he gets his wish, sort of. Elijah is one of a tiny handful of people in the Bible who don't die; rather he gets swooped off up into Heaven in a fiery chariot. This week my daughter—she's the lady who read the lessons today—my daughter and I went up to Tepoztlán and visited the monastery church where those restored frescoes in the dome of the apse show that very moment. Elijah in a flaming horse-drawn chariot racing up the Heavenly way, while his cloak falls to the ground and into Elisha's keeping. Elisha, now, he's a new figure in that story. The same way Elijah sort of came up out of nowhere, Elisha appears and becomes the old man's more or less assistant, though their relationship seems a little . . . cloudy. Notice how every time Elisha says he'll follow Elijah, the senior prophet waves him off. He promises to follow him to Bethel: Nah, best you stay here. Then to Jordan: I've got this, stand back. Then to the Jordan: Elisha hanging on for dear life. Finally when it looks like Elijah is sure enough on the way up and out, he asks Elisha what he'd like, and Elisha asks for a double portion of the old man's spirit, maybe a veiled suggestion that he could do twice as much as his predecessor. In any case, the mantle falls, Elisha shoulders it . . . and the faith in Yahweh survives. A wonderful hymn sung at ordinations memorializes the scene, *Elijah's mantle o'er Elisha cast*. Among many things we might learn from this, one stands out for me this morning: God's purposes are long, and nobody gets the whole job done in his own lifetime. How hard it is for us to remember that we are just passing along, that we don't get to finish the job and sit down and take the credit. As I see the end of the line drawing nearer for me, I often feel that somehow I have failed because I haven't worked everything out so my kids and grandkids will be all safe and sound; and then I remember that my parents and grandparents didn't leave it all worked out for me either, so not only does this teach us that the faith is not ours to keep but rather something we carry a while, then hand on; but also it helps us remember, it ain't about us. It's about God and his household, in which we are lucky to be the lowliest doorkeepers. If we can manage just that much, that's apostolic succession, no matter what shape it takes, and we here today are right smack in the middle of it.

The collect has a second half, of course, where we ask God to join us together in unity of spirit so we may become a holy temple acceptable for God's kingdom. Let's turn to today's gospel lesson for some light. We pick the story up when Jesus changes the narrative. He senses it's time for him to cut to the chase: he sets his face to go to Jerusalem, and that way lies trouble. His disciples want him to stay in Samaria, mighty anxious about what going to Jerusalem might mean, but the Samaritans run him off. They don't want to get involved. When James and John want to burn them up, Jesus rebukes them and marches on, jaw set, face like flint. As he goes, someone promises to follow him, but Jesus tells him he doesn't know what he's saying: foxes have holes and birds have nests, but where I'm going you cannot hide. He calls another, who asks time off to bury his father. Jesus' answer seems unkind, but it means let the past be past, because I am going straight ahead. Another offers to follow just as soon as he says his farewells at home. Jesus comes back with that killer line, "No one who puts a hand to the plow and looks back is fit for the kingdom of God." Wow. Takes your breath away, doesn't it? All the way through the Bible, people who look back get into trouble, most memorably Mrs. Lot. You remember, she looked back at Sodom and Gomorrah going up in flames and soon became wildly popular with all the livestock in the county, because she turned into a salt-lick. For us, this is a hard teaching. Jesus opts out of holing up with the Samaritans and taking it easy. His call is not to ease and self-congratulation but rather to self-denial, self-sacrifice. So much of what calls itself Christianity in the U.S. today is all about self-congratulation, a lovely kind of *bonum superadditum* to an already supremely self-satisfying life. I get tired of people telling me how blessed they are, makes me wonder how they can bear up under the glory. Jesus' call is to

Jerusalem and the cross. Glory comes later, and that's a whole lot of what we're up to right this red hot minute, picking up our cross and bearing it along behind the Master. We are indeed God's household, but that citizenship does not come without a price, without responsibility, including ours to become a holy temple fit for God's habitation and his kingdom.

Which takes us to Paul's letter. He says that Christ has indeed lifted the yoke of the law's slavery, but that doesn't free us up to sin ourselves silly. He casts it all in terms of flesh and spirit, and I take flesh to mean our unredeemed human nature, the way we act because of who we are, inheritors of a kind of moral blood disease that is hard to deal with. Paul tells the Galatians to live by the spirit, the Spirit of God, not by the flesh, and he gets right specific in that wonderful list of Bad Things that come from living by the flesh. I was a priest for seventeen years in the old Diocese of Dallas before Fort Worth spun off, and it was a big diocese, had at least 150 priests, maybe a couple hundred. And you know what they say about clergy. They're like manure: spread 'em out, and they do some good, but pile 'em up and they stink. And about every two or three years at diocesan convention, there'd be a stink, some priest doing something he shouldn't have, usually the one that heads that list, fornication in one form or another. The accusers would move a punishing resolution and bloviate and expostulate and righteous indignate for a while, and then Bishop Mason would say he'd support the resolution if they'd add the rest of the list. Let him who is without sin *etc*. But isn't it funny? That list starts with fornication, a real no no, but it goes on and on and on, and whereas we can all hike up our skirts and say we're not guilty of that, let's just move on down the line a little, okay? Impurity, licentiousness, fairly safe but maybe not pristine. Idolatry? Maybe not graven images, but a lot of us worship a lot of idols. Sorcery? Nobody I know of. Enmities? Strife? Jealousy? Not asking for a show of hands here. Anger? Oh Lord, I'd have to put my hand up for sure. Quarrels, dissensions, factions. Oh my. Envy? Drunkenness, carousing? I reckon you get the point, because I sure do. We spend just a whole lot of our lives wallowing around in a lot of that mire, don't we? As Paul says elsewhere, who will deliver me from this body of sin? The answer comes right up, the second list, and it starts with love, God's love for all of creation, Jesus' love for us, the love we are called by the Spirit to live in and share, a kind of *omnium gatherum* of all the rest. And the list goes on. Joy. Somewhere there's nostrum I can't quite recall, written by a nun, about how a sour-faced Christian is the devil's most effective tool. Just think how much a smile can do. Even if your feet hurt and you wish you were somewhere else, put a smile on your face and the whole game changes. Live joy and show it. After all, we Christians are the luckiest people on the face of the earth. Peace. St. Francis' prayer, Make me an instrument of thy peace. How many times in a day do we see little wars where maybe we could sow peace? We may get it back in our faces, yeah, but Jesus tells us to try. Patience. It took ten years living in Mexico to teach me patience. When I first moved down a good friend told me I needed to remember two things. First, in Mexico things take longer than they do. Yeah? Second, *mañana* does not mean tomorrow; it means not today. Just hold yer taters, Bub, it'll happen when it happens and not a minute sooner. Kindness. A kind word turneth away wrath. Generosity. We who live awash in things, how much do we share with people all around us who have almost nothing? Thank God for that food basket back there at the door. Faithfulness, not looking back. Gentleness, a soft touch instead of a fist. Self-control. Oh my. It all comes staring us right in the face, doesn't it. We are all too often right at home with so much in List One, yet come up short on List Two. At the end of the day, I'm usually thankful for a couple of things I got right and mighty ashamed of what I didn't, feel like most of the time I do about a forty-nine cent job of living, sometimes feel like Elijah, I give up, just let me crawl in a hole and pull it in after me. You ever feel that way?

I think we have three lessons here. First, our life in God is a matter of faith and discipleship which has been handed to us by someone and which we live with a while, then pass along. The job is not finished. Second, we must try to articulate that faith when called upon, but we teach far more effectively by example than by precept. I cannot forget that old saw, your life may be the only Bible your neighbor ever reads. Third, the salvation we live in is costly, demanding, dangerous in this wicked world, and we are truly earthen vessels, feeble, prone to wander, to leave the Lord we love. Where is the sweet gospel in all this?

Tell you a little story. My friend Owanah Anderson up in Wichita Falls puts out the best parish bulletin in the Anglican Communion, calls it JOYFUL Notes. Anticipating today's lessons, she published a little piece written by Vern Raschke, one of the priests that serves our little congregation up there. He had a German grandmother who was hard to get along with, grumpy, complaining, a little embarrassing. Evidently as she got old, she started carrying a bag around all the time, and wherever she went, she asked people for pieces of cloth or old worn out socks or torn shirts or maybe some stained napkins, whatever. Embarrassing. I mean, what would you do if that happened in your family. They just put up with it. Then one year at Christmas, everybody was handing out gifts and opening them and carrying on the way we do, when all of a sudden Grumpy Grandmaw said she had a gift for everybody. Lord, they wondered, what on earth? And then the old woman reached in her rag bag and pulled out and unfolded an absolutely gorgeous quilt in which everyone there recognized an old scarf that went out of style or a tie that once had gravy on it or a bit of an old lace hanky, just bits and pieces of their old lives, cast off things, things they no longer valued, were a little ashamed of, all cleaned up and stitched together with love and patience and love and a new vision and love and restored value and love, all made new and splendid, a new creation. Yeah, it's a little saccharine, I know, but isn't it just what the collect asks for, that God will bind us all together in love so that our forty-nine cent lives are made new and splendid and costly and rare, a temple fit for God's habitation and his kingdom? Yes indeed, little flock, yes indeed.

Amen.

3 July 2016

Seventh Sunday after Pentecost

2 Kings 5:1-14 Psalm 30 Galatians 6:1-16 Luke 10:1-11, 16-20

If you recall, last Sunday's collect and lessons were all about the apostolic succession of Christ's ministry, and we spent a little time on that ecclesiastical concept, then moved on beyond doctrine to consider what the readings taught about how faith is actually handed from believer to believer. Today we are asked to think about being apostles ourselves, and I'd bet not many of us ordinarily think of ourselves that way. I mean, apostles are those guys in the New Testament or to some degree the church's bishops down through the years, no? We're baptized and confirmed, most of us, but how does that make us apostles?

How many of you have been around this church long enough to remember when every eucharist started with the Summary of the Law? Hear what our Lord Jesus Christ saith. Thou shalt love the Lord thy God with all thy heart, and with all thy soul, and with all thy mind. This is the first and great commandment. And the second is like unto it: Thou shalt love thy neighbor as thyself. Upon these two commandments hang all the Law and the Prophets. Remember that? Well, today's collect reiterates exactly that. We acknowledge that God teaches us to keep all the commandments by loving him and our neighbor, and we ask for grace to carry out that immense work. Amen. What might slip one's attention is that, though we'd all agree that we believe that, accept it, know it by heart, we might not be quite so quick to realize how all that involves doing as well as saying, that the summary includes not only a statement of belief but a call to action, to carry out God's work of loving ourselves and our neighbors. Saying is not doing; affirming is not achieving, yet we are called and sent—the English word apostle comes from the Greek verb apostolein, to send—we are called and sent to do and to achieve, to be apostles. That arresting thought should get our attention and rattle us a little. Let's look at the lessons for some help.

In the first lesson we pick up on the Elisha story we started last week when he inherited Elijah's mantle, and here he's involved with a feller called Naaman, and this Naaman, he is a Big Shot. A. Really. Big. Shot. He's the general of the army of the King of Aram and has won many a battle and made his boss everybody else's boss for miles around. Probably he considers himself the true power behind the throne, could put that puppet king off the throne just as quick as he put him on it, or keeps him on it, whatever. Naaman is a Big Shot, sitting pretty. But he's got a problem, a fairly serious one at that: he's a leper. Now, in the Bible leprosy can refer to anything from the heartbreak of psoriasis to the armadillo kind that rots you right down to little nubbins and can finally kill you. We're not sure what kind Naaman's got, but whatever it is, it's enough to make him unhappy and make everybody else talk about it, which is not the way a Big Shot likes things to be. The talk is common enough to come to the attention of a little Hebrew slave girl, the product of some battle Naaman won, and when she hears about it, she thinks of Elisha, the prophet in Samaria, and tells Mrs. Naaman, I know a man who can heal Naaman. That word gets back to Naaman, thence to the king of Aram who is all for it. He sends a letter to the King Joram in Israel (who ruled Samaria) and tells him to get Naaman healed, along with about six carloads of money and fancy duds and what not to show what a Big Shot Naaman is. Joram has a faint and a fallback. "He's picking a fight with me! Am I God? How am I going to cure leprosy?" Somehow Elisha gets wind of the king's predicament and says, "Bring it on" So Naaman and all the booty wagons go down to Elisha's digs and park outside and honk. Cagey Elisha doesn't go out but rather sends a servant who tells Naaman to go wash seven times in the Jordan River, then goes back inside. Well now. Naaman pitches a Big Shot fit. "Go wash in the Jordan River? What kind of an answer is that? There are plenty of rivers in Aram to wash in, and I'm supposed go skinny dipping in some little Hebrew creek? What kind of healer is this quack? You'd think he'd put on his feathery shaman suit and come out here and wave his hands around and say some absolomons and dance around and take on, get up and march around the breakfast table at the very least! Fap! Kaff!" When he settles down, his staff calls him out. "Dude. Get over yourself. If he asked you to stand on your head and stack BBs with boxing gloves on, you'd do it, wouldn't you? This man says he can heal you. Get your uniform off and get in the water." And he did. Sure enough, he came up looking like a high school quarterback, flesh like a young boy's. It's a great story, of course, but the point is clear: God's purpose for us has nothing to do with show and gesture, nothing about pomp and circumstance. It starts with making ourselves little, accepting the divine simplicity, and getting out of the way so God can work. No matter how bad the leprosy in our souls is, God has sent a man who can heal us once we quit telling him how to do his job and trust him.

Let's go on to the gospel story in Luke. Jesus sends his disciples on ahead of him in all the gospels, makes them apostles, the sent ones. In this version he warns them, says the world into which they are sent to proclaim the Kingdom is not a nice place, they'll be like lambs among wolves. Flannery O'Connor, one of my favorites, described her writing as the story of the work of grace in territory largely held by the devil. Great metaphor! They are to travel light, just one carry-on bag and barefoot at that! Don't go alone but in pairs, and don't talk to people along the way. Makes you think of those Mormon boys in their black britches and white shirts, doesn't it? Easy to poke fun at them, but at least they're giving it a try. And the message is simple: peace. Peace to this house and everybody in it. If there's a hearer there, that peace will return to you; if not, shake the dust off your feet and keep moving. It's not your business to punish those who won't listen, to hassle them until they give in, none of that; but on your way out say, "The Kingdom of God has come near you." You are not the judge; you are the messenger, and the message is peace on the front end and peace on the back end. "I know a man who can heal you." It's not about you. It's about the Father and about me. So they went and guess what? It worked. They had a great time, even the spirits, whatever they were, submitted to them. When they tell Jesus, he exults. "Good job, guys. I can see the devil falling right off his throne! The power I give you will overcome all the snakes and scorpions the world can throw at you. But don't get chesty about it, okay? Don't boast about the results. Just be glad your names are written in the Kingdom of Heaven." What we find out in this lesson is that, such as they were—the disciples weren't much shakes—such as they were, the power of Jesus' message which is the love of God in the flesh is enough to overcome all the world's leprosy. Jesus is the man who can heal it. The hitch is, as he said at the outset, the fields are white to the harvest, but the laborers are few. We've got what it takes, but we often lack the gumption to get up and go do it. So here we are, then. We acknowledge that we have been sent, that we are God's apostles right here in this day and in this place, but we harbor doubts about ourselves. I mean, me? You want someone like me to go proclaim God's perfect kingdom? Look at me. Can't you see I've got leprosy? When are you going to make me perfect, because until I get over all this spiritual rash, I just don't think I can manage it. We've all got some Naaman in us, don't we? Well, that excuse won't wash, so to speak. We are sent and no two ways about it. So how does a leper like me proclaim the Kingdom of God, exactly? I need help.

The end of Paul's letter to the Galatians is pure practical instruction. He's assured them that God has freed them, healed them, and sent them to live out the gospel they believe. Some are going to be preachers, re-tell the story; but most are going to teach more by example than by precept, by doing the gospel to others, especially to those of the household of the faith but also to those whose faith needs a hand along the way. Look at the list. When our brothers and sisters mess up and fail their calling, don't shame them. Forgive them, just like God does. And while you're at it, watch your own step, lest you fall into sin yourself. When someone is in trouble, doesn't say what kind, you make it your trouble too. Go to them gently and offer to help if you can, at least let them know you care. Like that little slave girl, I know a man who can heal you. You may get it right back in your face, but don't take it personally. Just do it. And don't be a Naaman, puffed up with your own importance; rather examine your conscience at the end of a day, hold yourself accountable instead of changing the subject and talking about somebody else's sins. Never be weary in good works. The job is never done, so just keep at it. And finally don't be boastful. We don't have to tell people how blessed we are. They'll know it when they see it. What we boast of is Christ's gift of himself to the world. Now, those are very specific instructions, and if we can manage even a tolerable amount of that—we'll fail often enough, to be sure, since we've all got some leprosy left—then peace will be upon us and mercy, since we are the Israel of God. What else do we want? We know a man who can heal us.

Three lessons here, I think. First, God's purpose for us is simplicity itself, that we love him and ourselves and others, and he has sent a man who can heal us. That cuts through all the leprosy we can plead, makes as fresh as newborn babes, a new creation in our baptism into Christ Jesus. Second, our incorporation into Christ Jesus includes taking on the work he came to start. We are apostles, sin speckled and spotted as we are, and we are sent to proclaim peace, that God's Kingdom has come near, sometimes by precept but far more often by example, by doing, by carrying out the work of reconciliation. Third, we can't waste time boasting about all this good news that has overtaken us. Instead we need to spend the time we've got left rejoicing that our names are written in God's Heavenly Kingdom—and acting like it.

So apostles, let's finish our prayers today and then be about it. When you wake up in the morning, don't take a look in the mirror that shows all your leprosy and mutter, "Good God. Morning!" Instead look into the sunlight and smile and say, "Good morning, God! Your apostle is awake and ready to work. Send me."

Amen

The high altar at Cuernavaca's Roman Catholic cathedral, built by Cortéz. In 1957 the building was stripped to the inner walls, revealing murals painted by Indians. The gilt apse wall gleams mystically. Striking modern appointments reflect ancient design motifs. The lamps symbolize the seven gifts of the Holy Spirit. Do you see the palms of God's hands in the ceiling of the baldacchino?

10 July 2016

Eighth Sunday after Pentecost

Amos 7:7-17   Psalm 82   Colossians 1:1-14   Luke 10:25-37

    Boy! Today's collect is really a one-size-fits-all unit, isn't it? Do you remember what you said Amen to a few minutes ago? We asked God to hear us when we pray, to help us know and understand what we ought to do, and then for the grace and power to do it. What else do we need? God, show us what you want us to do and give us the power to do it. Isn't that a prayer anybody in any religion could say Amen to? Though I might want to add a word. My friend Katie Sherrod—she's the wife of Fr. Pool who was rector here years ago—wrote a book about the gutsy women who helped build Fort Worth. She called it *Grace & Gumption*. You look gumption up and you get synonyms like initiative, courage, resourcefulness, guts. I like that because it takes us beyond knowing and believing and accepting God's purpose for us and on down the road to doing something about it. It's a prayer we should always have at the center of our lives in God, because . . . y'know? . . . at times it's pretty hard to figure out what's going on, much less how we should act, and I don't know about you, but for me this past week has been a real doozy. If you've been watching the news, you know what I mean. I need help figuring out how to behave in the face of events today, and I expect living that out will require considerable gumption.

    Let's look at the lessons. We've been following the Old Testament prophets the past few weeks, and we've dealt with Elijah and Elisha, a couple of pretty spooky guys, dangerous at times, always elusive and shifty, either chopping up livestock and Baal prophets or running for their lives. Today we meet a new kind of prophet, Amos, and he wrote his inspirations down. We have his word for it, not a second hand account, and that's new. (Let me stop here and say something about Old Testament prophets and prophecy *per se*. Prophets are not crystal ball gazers who fall into a trance and predict the future. Rather they are men who see the present so intensely and perceptively that the shape of the future becomes apparent. They look at current events and say, "You keep this kind of madness up, and this is what's going to come of it." It's what any of us can do and in fact do a lot of the time; but the Old Testament prophets did it in circumstances which made it mortally dangerous. They spoke truth to the power structure of their time; it got them all killed.) So back to Amos. Amos lived in what looked like good times. Both the north (Israel) and the south (Judah) were at peace, prosperous, lots of trade, plenty of money floating around. In Israel King Jeroboam II was fat and happy and in cahoots with the seriously corrupt religious establishment. Right. Any time you see the state and the church getting chummy, skeet for the woodshed, run for the hills, the dam has bust. A theocracy is about the most dangerous thing going, because usually it means that the state has the church bought and sold. Whatever the state does is God's will. After all, God has been on the side of every army that ever went to war, which must have been particularly poignant in the American Revolution in places like Virginia where both armies were Anglican! And that was the situation Amos lived in. The state tolerated a good bit of non-Yahweh religion, "the high places of Isaac," Baal shrines;

and the church winked while the rich squeezed the poor to death. Bad stuff. And you notice also that when the king tells him to go prophesy somewhere else, he right quick distances himself from that: "I'm not a prophet, not part of that crowd. I'm a farmer." (I learned, by the way, something about that "dresser of sycamore trees" bit. Evidently there's a sycamore in that part of the world that bears figs. Did anybody know that? I didn't.) Well anyhoo, Amos' world is going to Hell by the short road, and he has the gumption to call it out—social injustice, religious hypocrisy, moral turpitude, all of it. "God," says Amos, "is going to drop a plumb line on Israel and straighten it out, just like we use a plumb line to build a straight wall. You are acting like Hell, and it's going to be Hell to pay."

Well, I've got to ask, does that sound anything like today? Just look around us. It's not all in the U.S. England just took a vote to do something pretty far-reaching, and now they're not at all sure they're happy about it, everybody running for cover. And in the rest of Europe, people are choosing up sides. Germany's getting antsy about immigrants, France is one step away from a pogrom. In the United States, we see police shooting black men one day and a black man shooting police the next, and leaders of both sides of the argument are talking right past each other. One side says we have to have stronger gun laws; the other side says we have to have stricter law enforcement; the people in the middle don't know which way to turn. It's all through what we call Western Culture, Europe and the Americas, and Mexico is by no means exempt. You know the old saying, *Ay México, tan lejos de diós y tan cerca a los Estados Unidos!* What happens in the *país vecino al norte* is going to wash over into Mexico. And vice versa. We're all in the same tub, and it's a slop bucket. And how do our leaders respond? I get sick of hearing people say, "Well, moments like this bring us together." Really? I don't see that. I see us being shredded. And is that the only way we can be brought together, in fear and hatred of an enemy? Is that the best we have? I want to yell when somebody asks for "a moment of silence." A moment of silence indeed. What we need is forty days of fasting and prayer, though I don't think anybody will call for that. Was it ever any better? Somehow I kind of think so. When I was a kid, things seemed more civil. Not everybody was an enemy. My Grandmother Yeager's highest praise was to call us good citizens. But somewhere along the line, about fifty years ago or so I remember out of almost nowhere a torrent of the literature of self-affirmation flooding the bookstores, all about how wonderful we all are, how we can do anything we want (a dangerous lie), how we must assert ourselves. Lord, I believe in giving children a good self-image and having one for ourselves, but not that bunch of self-absorption. I remember when I came back to Texas after ten years in Mexico, when I watched television with my mother all I saw were ads for drugs. "Does your eyelid twitch sometimes. You may have Twitchy Eyelid Syndrome. TES! Ask your doctor if you're ready for Lidstill." And that's gotten worse. Or ads about managing wealth, that in a country where about half the population lives right at the poverty line. Drugs and money. And today it's all about "getting the service you deserve," "taking control," "earning points or miles or whatever." It's sickening. And the saddest part is, we swill it all up like hogs at a trough. When do we hear about giving and caring for each other? Every now and then somebody talks about "giving back," but that's usually the crumbs that fall from the rich man's table. Thank God for David Brooks. I don't know how many of you know him. He's a syndicated columnist, appears in *The Wall*

Street Journal and *The New York Times*. He's Jewish, but I think if you scratch him you find a man on the verge of conversion to Christianity, quotes St. John and other Christian writers all the time. The other day he did an article on altruism, behavior that helps others, benefits others with no expectation of reward. He reported studies showing that small children, two-year-olds say, who see someone drop a clothes pin will automatically pick it up and try to give it back. Natural response. Help others. But if they are rewarded, the next time that happens, they'll be less apt to help, because they've learned to ask What's in it for me? His point was that altruism seems to be part of our nature until we teach ourselves to be ulterior. I've said often about myself, there's not an altruistic bone in my body; I'm the most ulterior person I know. Where did I learn that? Where do we all learn to expect the worst from ourselves? Well, that's enough harangue, but I think it's pretty clear we are in trouble, serious trouble, and life is about to . . . When my Grandmother Yeager was a child, she said she and her sibs liked to shuck corn by pulling it through a knothole in a plank, just skins the husk right off. Well, life is about to jerk us through a knothole. Where is help? Dear God, show us what to do!

What blessed irony that today's gospel is Luke's parable of the Good Samaritan, an epiphanic coincidence. What's the antidote to all that poison we just choked on? Take care of each other. Simple as that. Stop seeing each other as adversaries or as prey but rather as partners, brothers and sisters, neighbors. You know the story by heart. A pesky lawyer is chopping logic with Jesus, always a losing proposition, asks who is in fact his neighbor. Then comes the story. A fellow falls among thieves on the road, gets knocked in the head, robbed, thrown in the barrow ditch, and left for dead. Along comes a priest on his way to church, and God knows he doesn't want to get involved and messed up and impure, so he passes by on the other side. Next a Levite, the reader and acolyte, same story, he passes by on the other side. And then a low down, good for nothin', heretical, Not One Of Us Samaritan, comes by and lo and behold goes right over to the bloody wretch, gives him First Aid, puts him in the back of his CRV, drives him to the Holiday Inn, checks him in, leaves his American Express card at the desk, says he'll pick it and the tab up next time he comes that way. Jesus then extorts the right answer from his questioner, and says, "Go and do thou likewise." How plain can it be? And yet how do we in fact usually treat each other? I've told you this story before, but it fits. One Sunday morning at home I was on my way to Trinity Church to say Mass, a cold morning, windy, spitting rain. I was driving across a long bridge over the Trinity River and spotted an old man, older than me, shuffling along under a backpack about the size of my car, having a hard time in the wind. What should I have done? Yes, pull over, ask if I could give him a lift anywhere. But no, this priest had places to go and things to do, and I passed by on the other side. I know all the reasons why that was the sensible thing to do, and I'm not going to commit hara kiri over it; but it is so typical of the way we react to people in distress, don't want to get involved, just slither by on the other side. It's in our DNA somehow, and we're not going to improve much. But the point is blindingly clear, and without further elaboration, I commend the matter to your conscience. We all need to re-program.

Mercy, where's the sweet gospel this morning? Let's turn to Paul and today's lesson from Colossians. You've heard me say that reading Paul is often like listening to Stravinsky, everybody against everybody, especially when he's trying to explain things. Well, not this morning. How many of you remember Amadeus? Do you remember the scene when Salieri, Mozart's rival, finds a manuscript of a composition not yet performed, just on paper in Mozart's own hand? He imagines the music, and the most beatific look comes over his face. He can hardly speak. He chokes out, "It was like hearing the voice of God." Well, that's what the lesson sounds like this morning, the voice of God speaking love to his children. "I have heard of your faith in Christ Jesus . . . the faith of the gospel you have heard . . . how it and you are bearing fruit . . . how you understand my grace . . . I want you filled with knowledge of my will in wisdom and understanding . . . leading lives worthy of me, bearing fruit in good works . . . being strong so you can live through anything . . . in the Kingdom of my Son who has given you forgiveness for all your sins." Wow. That's the way God sees his children, the way God sees us here this morning, his children gathered to learn from him what he gives us and what he hopes for us, as well as the grace and strength and gumption to live out his expectation that we live up to Jesus' teaching in that parable with each other and with every other battered soul our Father in Heaven puts across our path. You see, God believes in us. It's up to us to see that, believe it, and live accordingly. What could be sweeter than that?

I see three lessons for us this morning. First, we are in trouble. Oh, we've always been in trouble, but today, right now, the walls seem to be closing in. How are we to act as baptized people? I heard someone say this week, "Oh, we live in paradise here in Cuernavaca. None of this touches me. I just go inside and close the door, and it all goes away." That's a delusion. Opting out is not an option, not for me anyway. This is the nest we've made for ourselves, and it's ours to clean up. I can't do it all, to be sure, but nobody but I can do my part, so I'm resolved to try. I hope you will too. Second, the solution is right in front of us: take care of each other. I can't take care of every battered soul, but I can at least offer a lift to those I find on the same bridge with me. I hope you will too. Third, I know what God wants of me. It's in today's gospel lesson. I just need somehow to open up so God can give me the gumption to go and do likewise. I hope you will too.

Amen.

Here Avenida Humboldt dives down to meet Calle Salazar as the Amanaco *barranca* cleaves the city's throbbing heart. The central market and bus terminal are just beyond to the right. The sidewalks are often staircases to help pedestrians manage the steep inclines. Locals say walking in Cuernavaca will "put a leg on ya." *Caminar en Cuernavaca te pone pierna.*

17 July 2016

Ninth Sunday after Pentecost

Amos 8:1-12 Psalm 52 Colossians 1:15-28 Luke 10:38-42

How many of you remember the way we used to baptize people in the Episcopal Church? It was never done at the main service on Sunday morning, or at least I never saw it that way. Rather we did it after the service, just the family and godparents and close friends, very private, very family. Priests wore a stole that was purple on one side, white on the other, and the renunciations were done with the purple side out. Then for the baptism, you'd switch it to white. It was in a way something nice we did with babies and something we did rather hurriedly for an adult who had put it off too long! And when it was all over, we went to the Country Club for lunch. I remember recalling once that when he was baptized, Jesus didn't go to the Country Club. He went out into the desert to deal with the devil. Well whatever. But thank God the Liturgical Movement of the last century transformed all that. The Prayer Book rite we use this morning regains baptism as a joint venture between a congregation and God, an extended family affair in which you will have a lot to do before all's said and done this morning.

Let me say something about baptism in general. I think I see three things going on in baptism. The first is repentance. Now, usually we take repentance to mean feeling very sorry about what we just got caught doing. That's not repentance; that's guilt, and guilt does not always include a change of attitude, though it does include a whole lot of regret about not getting by with whatever mischief we were up to. Repentance is a whole lot more than that. The word's Latin roots include a sense of regret, even punishment, but also a sense of doing over, re-doing, as in *pentimento*, when a painter covers an earlier image with a new one. The Hebrew word that occurs in the Old Testament is *shuv*, and that means to turn around and go the other way, to look in another direction. What it means for Christians is to stop believing Satan's lies about us and start believing God's truth about us. The Father of Lies has always told us that we're not much shakes, that we can't do anything good, that we may as well crawl in a hole and pull it in after us and that's where he'll come looking for us. But that's a lie. God created us for glory, though we invariably fall short of it. We call that shortfall sin, and albeit we don't really know what it is, we know it's there—our weakness or our foolishness or our wickedness or the fateful shake of the potter's hand. We just know it's there. But we see the glory God intends for us revealed in Christ Jesus, and that is the truth. So repentance for us means more than regret; it means getting a new vision, a new pair of eyes, a new way of grasping the divine reality and our inheritance in it. Well, the guy on the front row has repented, of what it's not ours to ask, but he has asked to be baptized as a sign of that repentance.

Second is mystery because we're talking about death and resurrection. Mystery does not mean smoke and mirrors; rather mystery is experience that transcends words, can be apprehended but not comprehended, shared only partly with others though recognizable to all who have known it. Mystery is where we are when we glimpse the hem of God's garment. St. Paul tells that in baptism we die with Christ and are raised with him in his resurrected life—and that is a mystery, the central mystery of Christian faith. Don't expect me to tell you how it works, because I have absolutely no idea. I once had a parishioner who cared for her not-quite-all-there nephew. He was in his thirties, could hold a job at Goodwill, but he wasn't wired right. Somehow I learned he was not baptized, asked her why not. "Fr. So-and-So would not baptize him," she told me, "said he wouldn't understand what was happening." Lord God. I at once confessed that I didn't understand what was happening, I just knew that it happened. We baptized him. The old fashioned Baptist preachers were good on this. If you've ever been in a vintage Baptist church in my part of the world, you know there's always an elaborate baptistery on the wall behind the pulpit, a glass wall so you can see, a tank of water big enough for two adults, plus a painting of some pious lady's notion of the River Jordan—though most of them I've seen look more like the country out around Sweetwater. The preacher, all got up in a white gown, and the candidate, usually got up in another white gown, both go down into the water. And, the preacher assures you, a third party goes into the water too: Jesus. I like that a lot, and what Jesus does in that water I can't tell you, but I know what comes out—a sopping wet preacher and a brand new member of the Body of Christ, washed by the Lamb in the waters of forgiveness. We Anglicans don't usually baptize by immersion, but it's available if someone wants it. I've baptized in rivers, in a swimming pool or two, once even in a bathtub because somebody wanted it. What counts after all is the water, the sign of washing and making new. There's an Alka Seltzer ad I've seen that says you don't have to drink all the sediment at the bottom of the glass, because the medicine's in the water. I like that too. Jesus is in the water, and he's the medicine that heals our sin sick souls. We about to put Jesus water on our brother on the front pew.

Third, there's incorporation. We're initiating Siegfried today, making him one of the club, accepting him publicly as One Of Us, part of the extended family that includes all of us and every person who was ever baptized and those who will be until we all come to our eternal destiny. Not only that, we are commissioning him to live a life worthy of his baptism, avoiding sin when he can, repenting when he can't, accepting forgiveness, and getting back to the job of worship and proclamation and service to the needy souls and bodies life brings his way. In all that we say, again with St. Paul, that he will be clothed in Christ, that the baptismal garment he wears today will be made fuller and richer and more glistening every day until he is whiter than any fuller's soap could make him. Jesus will give him the garment, and the Holy Spirit will make it splendid enough for the divine habitations, just as is happening to each of us here today and to all God's chillen on their way to life eternal with God.

I think we have to look at the lessons briefly. They didn't know they were going to be involved in a baptism, but there's plenty of baptismal language in them, even in that scary passage from Amos. After all the denunciations and dire promises, the very last line points straight at what we're doing today. Amos speaks of a famine, a famine for truth, of a people seeking the word of the Lord, starving for it but not finding it. Well, in Christ Jesus we believe we have found that word, the incarnate Word, Jesus the Christ, and we believe that in finding him, we find truth. Our brother up front has sought and has found. In Luke's gospel, we read the story of two women. Martha is all about getting things done; Mary is all about being quiet and listening. In all old fashioned Episcopal Churches you used to have a St. Martha's Guild, the hot, sweaty ladies in the kitchen who set up the parish hall, put out the plates and silver, brought the food or cooked it there, served it, then stayed back in the kitchen and washed the dishes after everybody else went home. The St. Mary's Guild were the ladies who did the flowers, tended the altar, washed and ironed the linens, sewed vestments, and generally made the surroundings lovely. Not a little animosity reigned between the two groups at times, one all about doing, the other all about hearing and enjoying. Luke knew that life in Christ is about both. Last week's gospel showed us the Good Samaritan and Jesus' commandment: Go and do likewise. Today he balances that brilliantly. Today he tells the action packed Martha, sit and listen. In baptism we are about both: we wash and anoint, but we also listen for the rush of angels' wings as a soul is born anew into Christ Jesus. And let's not forget, we also enjoy it, we take joy in it. There's a whole lot about the gospel of Jesus that points to joy, to the exhilarating breath of the Holy Spirit dwelling with us right now in the beauty of holiness. We are going to enjoy baptizing our new brother. Finally, there's that glorious language in Colossians where we read that Jesus is "the image of the invisible God, the firstborn of all creation" in whom we see all the glory of the Father. He is both our redeemer and our model, and he will give to us all that the Father has given him, will clothe us in himself, so that in the last day God will see us made perfect and splendid in Jesus his son, "holy and blameless and irreproachable before him."

All right. Today we are a people seeking the truth. We believe we have found it in Jesus. We believe that in the waters of baptism we have died with him and are made alive in his resurrected body. We believe that we are being clothed by Jesus in the Holy Spirit with the joyous wedding garment of the bride of Christ. In that faith, we come before the Holy Trinity to welcome God's newest resurrected child. That said, let's get it done.

Amen.

Tropical birds in the garden at the iconic Las Mañanitas hotel, one of Cuernavaca's must-see venues for over sixty years. Once a private residence, the complex now houses a large hotel with meeting spaces and other amenities, plus an *al fresco* restaurant. The spacious gardens feature monumental statuary by twentieth-century Mexican artist Francisco Zúñiga, and peacocks and other tropical birds roam the grounds or perch contentedly, well fed. Sadly the food and service have declined recently, though it's still not to be missed if you visit. Have a drink, then eat at Gusto in Acapantzingo, a charming neighborhood just across the Amanaco *barranca* from downtown.

24 July 2016

Tenth Sunday after Pentecost

Hosea 1:2-10   Psalm 85   Colossians 2:6-19   Luke 11:1-13

When I first looked at the lessons for this morning I found them . . . dicey, I suppose, rather difficult to get a handle on. The collect and all three lessons offer dozens of opportunities for development and exploration, enough for a couple dozen sermons at least. The Spanish word *canijo* suggested itself to me, but I'm told that's a bad word, means puny or skimpy, which they are not, but also difficult. So I'll just settle for dicey. I mean, just look at the collect. It speaks of God as our protector, as the one who makes everything, including us, strong and holy, our guide through things temporal and our assurance of things eternal. I mean, there's a lot there to dwell on. But that's not what we're going to do.

Next, Hosea, another of those grimsome and gruesome Old Testament prophets we've been working through lately, and he's no exception. He opens up with another bad word, whoredom, that moment when people take the most beautiful and intimate relations and cheapen and sully them for money, in essence says that the northern kingdom, Israel, has whored its relation with God for mere gain. I recently a book by P.J. O'Rourke called *A Parliament of Whores*, all about the U.S. government in the 1980s, and it sure wasn't a pretty picture. Yet even at the end of this smelly condemnation, there comes a promise, a time when the people of Israel, redeemed from their prostitution, will once more be like the sands of the sea and called the "children of the living God." So no matter how they've mucked up things temporal, they still will one day inherit things eternal. And so they did.

Next Colossians. Although in history it actually comes after the gospel, the way we arrange the lessons, it comes next, and it is a proclamation of the triumph the end of the Hosea lesson promises. Paul—or whoever wrote it, scholars disagree—admonishes the flock not to abandon the victory they have in Christ Jesus, warns them about getting caught up in "philosophy and empty deceit," reminds them of their freedom from the old law and their new resurrected life in Jesus, dismisses worries about keeping feasts and fasts and religious falderal. He's reacting to what we know as Gnosticism, a religious attitude which moved in on early Christianity before they had quite figured out how they were to live. Gnosticism essentially says, Jesus is not enough, that there is a great curtain of unknowing between us and God's ultimate reality—and we know where the peep hole is. You have to have special knowing, gnosis, for salvation. The writer warns them against that side-track, urges them to hold fast to Jesus, the head of the body of which they are all part. This is a lesson from a position of strength, of victory won.

And then the gospel lesson from Luke, and it is a bombshell. The disciples come to Jesus and say, "Teach us to pray." Then follows Luke's version of the Our Father and a flourish of images depicting a doting father, lavishing gift after gift upon his children, the apples of the divine eye, avidly ladling out his greatest gift, the Holy Spirit to those who ask, seek, knock. Well, with that I knew where we should turn our minds and hearts today: the whole mysterious and wonderful world of prayer, and there's enough there for countless forty-five minute sermons, though I know you all want me to think in terms of twelve! Let me tell you, you can't even read the Wikipedia article on prayer in twelve minutes. We can hardly do more than scratch the surface this morning, so what I hope to do is just go opening a bunch of windows and inviting your gaze, hoping that something will stick and that on your own you'll chase some of those bunny tails down the trails they signal. I won't cover it all, likely won't mention some things you'd like to hear, but I'll do my best to hit the high spots and then turn more specifically to the Lord's Prayer.

I used to read philosophy a good bit, thought philosophers had the answers. I've got a copy of Bertrand Russell's *History of Western Philosophy* in my little library, turn to it often. But what I concluded after a while is that philosophers don't have answers; rather they raise questions. What I see is, they take a question and cut it in half, then drop one half and take up the other. Then they cut that in half, drop one half, and on and on and on until the whole thing is so thin you can see through it. So I gave it up . . . although about fifteen years ago I did read a book by Paul Woodruff, philosophy professor at the University of Texas, called *Reverence: Renewing a Forgotten Virtue*. His subject was how in the U.S. people have lost a sense of reverence, and it was fairly interesting. But one sentence in particular leapt out at me. In a discussion of various religious beliefs, he wrote: "Deities come and deities go; prayer remains." Wow. Through all humankind's history of seeking God, conceptions of deity come and go; but we and our forebears have always prayed. That thought really expanded my grasp on prayer. Evidently every human society we are aware of, from the very earliest, long before writing or history, known to us only in archaeology, right up to our own—they all have had some sense of the presence of something beyond the evidently physical in the cosmos and have all left evidence that in their many ways, they tried to reach that presence, to communicate with it. Sometimes it was wonderful, sometimes horrible, terrifying, but they believed it was there, and they wanted to speak to it, hear from it And evidently ever since we have had language, we have been trying to speak not only to each other but also to the great Transcendent Someone we sense Out There. It all begins with wonder.

That brings up the whole matter of mind, because we communicate with our minds. Does God have a mind? We think we are made in God's image, so I figure something like our mind must be a part of God. The omnipresent urge to communicate with God—let's just use that word—also implies that God wants to communicate with us, seems to have built the urge to speak with one another into us. Is prayer then communication with God? I think so. Tennessee Williams is a funny source for a preacher, but in a letter he wrote once about how his health was beginning to fail he notes how these little rubbery machines we live in betray us in the long run; but he says that inside these little machines there is a tenant, a someone, and that tenant is always looking out, trying to speak to someone. I like that image, think it suits prayer.

But then . . . if we all pray, how do we pray? Is there A Way to Pray? I recall once going to the opening session of a parish prayer study. The leader opened up at once with: "There are five fingers of prayer: confession, petition, intercession, thanksgiving, and praise." Wow, I thought, aren't we getting the cart before the horse? If I were leading a group studying prayer, I think I'd open with, "Tell me if you pray, and if you do, how you pray." Every single person who prays, prays in some ways unlike anyone else, because we are all unique, we each know God as God knows us, one by one by one. Yet we all pray alike in some respects. Those "five fingers" are just one way of thinking of very traditional Christian prayer and might make no sense at all to people of other faith.

Is prayer transactional? Is there a *quid pro quo*? Do we have to say enough prayers to change God's mind or earn some reward? Some schools of prayer think so, and the Latin root for prayer implies asking for something specific. The Spanish *pedir* comes from that. But the Hebrew root for prayer implies something more like a self-examination, a kind of spiritual check-up, even a conversation with God. "How am I doing?" And the Jewish tradition does not hesitate a bit to get into an argument with God. "How long, O Lord, how long?" Is prayer aimed at changing God's purpose? Or is meant to change us? C.S. Lewis tells a story of a friend who at last married his true love after a long, long courtship which seemed hopeless, told his friend he knew the wedding was an answer to prayer. His friend replied, "Oh, no. I don't pray to change God. I pray to change myself."

So far we've touched on noisy prayer. We Episcopalians make a lot of racket when we pray together, and you know I like hearty responses and lusty singing. Yet other traditions, including the Quakers who worship in silence, believe that prayer is a kind of emptying of the mind and the soul so God can speak to us. Buddhist prayer is about that much of the time. Perhaps that's part of the difference between private prayer and common prayer. Jesus told us to go into our closets and close the door, not to babble like the pagans or put on long robes—like these I'm wearing—and carry on when we pray. Even people of no faith practice transcendental meditation; and in the Christian tradition, the Taizé community, founded in France in the last century, has offered a kind of worship where people simply come into a sacred space and pray quietly. There may be candles, may be simple, repetitive music, a kind of melodic mantra, but it's not exactly *common* worship, more like worship *in community,* where each one is free to come and pray, then go. Many parishes in the U.S. now offer Taizé worship, including at least two in Fort Worth.

Is common prayer, when we're all of one mind and one spirit (more or less) an attempt somehow to harness the power of God the Holy Spirit? If you've ever been to a high school football game in Texas, you know about the power of spirit. It's the homecoming game, the score is tied, the ball's on the three yard-line, it's fourth down, ten seconds to go in the game. The teams face off, and up in the stands on this side, ten thousand souls are united as one, on the other, ten thousand more united the other way. You can feel the power of it. Remember that this day literally millions of Christians of catholic heritage and lot of reformed protestantism are praying the same prayers, pondering these same lessons. You'd think that would have some effect, and surely it does. The trouble, of course, is that the minute we end our exploration of things eternal and walk out the door, we are back in the middle of things temporal where we are not always equal to the struggle.

Think also of the irony of the way we often approach prayer. My friend at home, Fr. Sam McClain, has a wonderful bit where he describes us getting ready for our prayer routine, going to our own special place, lighting a candle or kneeling down or otherwise somehow assuming an attitude of prayer and then, in effect, saying, "Okay God, front and center. Sam

McClain is going to pray!" As if God weren't aware of us all the time? As if God doesn't know what we're thinking all the time?—which is a fairly daunting thought. That little drama has led me to think of myself in fact praying all the time, because I'm communicating with God all the time. And that's both comforting in a way and plenty unsettling in another.

What about when our prayers are "not answered"? What that usually means is that we don't get what we're asking for, and that can give rise to a sense of the absence of God—though that widely observed phenomenon itself, seems to me, points straight back to the built-in urge to seek God. I have a friend who prays very specifically. I mean, she puts in the commas and the periods, crosses the *t* and dots the *i* when she prays. Her daughter had a horrible marriage, lasted for over twenty years, her husband was just a sorry good-for-nothing so-and-so, a vile person. My friend prayed about it year after year after year, told God exactly how that marriage needed fixing. Finally the daughter divorced him, re-married and has been happy since. My friend said in amazement, "I can't believe how God worked that out in spite of my prayers." The thing is, what we pray for often isn't what we need; but God always gives us what we need. When prayers aren't answered, perhaps the prayers need changing. At times also there are things in our lives which, as one friend who'd lost two sons said, God is going to have to explain that to me. That's justified too, in my view.

Well, we could go on, but let's not. Instead let's turn to that prayer Jesus taught us and consider it in some detail. We begin by addressing God as Father. I know that bothers some people nowadays, but it's the way the Hebrew tradition addressed the creator God. I know people today, some priests, who pray Father/Mother God, which is okay with me. I don't think I'd like to pray to Parent, seems a little generic. But the point is, the relationship Jesus signals is intimate, close, from the cradle, from the womb, nay before the womb. It claims that we are God's children, and that is a large claim. Then we are told to think of God's name as holy. What is holy? Well, at least it's something that is not like us, something pure and flawless and mystically beyond us. In Jesus' mind that might also have had to do with the Old Testament name of God, Yahweh, the tetragrammaton too holy to be uttered. Though we don't think about that anymore, I do know that when I was a kid I could get slapped away from the table for doing what we called "taking God's name in vain," and you know what I mean. Here I think it means that we should think of God and everything connected with God in that awed reverence the philosopher said we have lost. Then we ask for God's Kingdom to come—and Matthew's version adds "thy will be done on earth as it is in Heaven." That means we recognize that God wants something to happen among us that hasn't yet fully happened, that we know God's Kingdom is unlike the temporal things we muddle through, and that we accept our responsibility to live lives that make us worthy of inheriting things eternal even while we are on the earth. Another large claim, another large mission. And that bit, Thy will be done. Now, that is hard! What is God's will, after all? It is that everything be done in love, everything. If we don't pray in love, act in love, then we don't mean that part. An easy example: we are to pray for our enemies, all right, and we do. But do we love them? Not usually, and until we do love our enemies, we will remain enemies. Then we let God know we need certain things to get through these things temporal, our daily bread. And when we ask for bread for ourselves, we accept the responsibility to share that bread with those who have less than we do—which is most of the people on the planet. Then we ask for God's forgiveness, claim we earn it by forgiving everyone who offends us. Do we? Finally we ask not to be brought to the test, because we know we're earthen vessels and are going to fail at least as often as we win the fight against the world, the flesh, and the devil. What a tiny little prayer, and what a vast, overwhelming freight of glory and mission it includes! And Jesus doesn't stop there. The prayer is a frightening assumption of power and glory, almost too daring to undertake, considering who we are. But Jesus reassures us that all we have to do is do it, just ask, just seek, just knock, because God will give, find, open, is literally dying to give us what we need. He all but jokes then: You guys are not anything to brag about, but you give your own children wonderful gifts. Why do you think God won't give you everything you need, all bound up in the Holy Spirit. All you have to do is do it!

What glory there is in that little bitty prayer, and what joy. There's something in the Lord's Prayer that points back to that primitive sense of pure wonder from which prayer springs. Have you ever watched those magnificent fireworks displays that happen in New York City and in Washington D.C. at New Year or the Fourth of July? Vast crowds gather in parks and along rivers, milling and chatting until night falls, and then glory opens up in the skies, showers of blazing light, lighting up the heavens. And from time to time the camera sweeps across the amazed faces in the crowd, and oh the exultation and exhilaration! I've often thought if some being from another planet who knew nothing about us witnessed such a scene and asked "What on earth are they doing?" the answer would be, "Why they're worshiping, they're praying." Prayer is humbling, no doubt about it, but it's also glorious, and I hope for all of you that there are moments in your life of prayer when you get a glimpse of the glory in the skies.

Well, I've got no snappy wrap-up for all this. The experience of prayer is not subject to summary in my view. I reckon the only way we can actually get it wrong is not to pray at all. So let's get back to it.

Amen.

31 July 2016

Eleventh Sunday after Pentecost

Hosea 11:1-11 Psalm 107:1-9, 43 Colossians 3:1-11 Luke 12:13-21

Isn't it wonderful this morning, after so many Sundays with such challenging lessons, to have a lectionary that lets us concentrate pretty purely on God's goodness and mercy? It certainly makes this preacher's job easier, easier and a lot more fun when I'm not called on to harangue the congregation quite so much. And today's collect and all the lessons draw our attention to God's sweet goodness—not to say there are not some stingers in there, but not the kind of scary stuff we've been hearing lately, especially from the Old Testament prophets, all about scouring God's people raw! Let's look at each in the order they come in.

The lovely collect, to which you said a very hearty Amen, asks that God's mercy both cleanse and protect his church, his people, you and me, us. How does God cleanse the church? I know some might take this to mean that God should purge the church of bad practices and bad belief, getting rid of heresy and all that. But you know? I think those are problems we worry about a lot more than God does, often a lot of falderal that proves fairly meaningless over time, even harmful. I'm not a Puritan. The way I see it, God cleanses his church from within, from all the things that separate us from God, that thing we don't always understand but always admit, from sin. And how does he do that? With forgiveness of course, his unceasing will to love us no matter what and, like the father of the Prodigal, to forgive us long before we actually ask for it. Some people see forgiveness as the result of repentance, that we have to feel really bad for a really long time before God finally relents and clears the record. Not me. I think repentance is not the pre-requisite of forgiveness but rather the result of it. I mean, don't you feel awful when you're misbehaving? I know I do, and often it's when I'm feeling like the devil that it finally dawns on me that maybe it's my own doing; and I check and sure enough, lots of the time all I have to do is some behavior modification, stop acting like hell to stop feeling like hell. God cleanses us that way, washes our innards, straightens us up, sends us on our way rejoicing. He cleanses us with goodness.

And how does God protect us? Well, certainly not from circumstances, because really horrible things happen to good people, to innocent people. There's a wonderful little boy eight years old out in the yard this morning, part of the family that will be helping set up and clean up here for the next couple of Sundays. He has hemophilia, bless his heart, no way his fault; and he's limping around because he fell and hurt his knee—little boys don't sit still—and bled so much, his doctor doesn't want him to straighten his leg because it will break open the scab and bleed again. My God! An innocent child, suffering. No, God doesn't seem to protect us that way. Rather I think he protects us from what's wrong within us, our weakness and foolishness and wickedness. He protects us by forgiving us and then encouraging us with his love and the Holy Spirit to live lives worthy of the Kingdom of Heaven, which among other things will straighten all bent legs and put smiles back on children's faces—although that little boy is already smiling. God protects us from ourselves, our laxity, prone to wander, prone to leave the God we love. He protects us with goodness.

Then the collect asks God to govern us, to rule us with goodness, and it seems to me that happens through the forgiveness and protection we asked for earlier. All our lives, when we are turned by God to accord with the divine love and mercy, are ruled by God's whole goodness.

Now Hosea. At last! At last we hear an Old Testament prophet speaking gently, tenderly, achingly. That's pretty rare in the Hebrew scriptures. I know that's the way they seem to have experienced God, but it's often so foreign to the loving God Jesus came to reveal. Today though it's all about the love of a mother, a father, for a child. Let's just run back through it in a hurry. "When Israel was a child, I loved him, called him." And of course, as you know if you've raised children, they don't always heed the call. It is irritating and sometimes heart-breaking. My son Stephen, who will come with his wife for a visit this week, was as rebellious as they get, and it was hard. But I love him like fire, and you go after him, you've got me to deal with. In this passage we hear that from God. "I taught Ephraim to walk, I carried them in my arms, healing them even when they didn't know . . . cords of human kindness, bands of love . . . lifted them to my cheek." Oh my. What's sweeter than a baby's breath? When I ran a department at the University of Monterrey, I had about fifty teachers, eighty per cent of them women, and though I couldn't see their area, I always knew when a baby or a picture of a baby had come in. Such oohing and aahing and cooing. The urge to pick up and cuddle, and it comes from God here in Hosea. And God's children are getting the rewards of their misbehavior, war and strife and the sword. Yet "How can I give you up, how can I hand you over like Admah and Zeboiim?" Those last two, by the way, were little towns adjacent to Sodom and Gomorrah. God recoils from it, his heart grows tender. "I am no mortal, I am God, and I will not come in wrath." How unlike us. Rather God will bring his children gently, "like trembling birds, like doves." I just don't see how it can get any sweeter than that. This passage doesn't deny circumstance; bad things are happening; but behind the cloud God stands keeping watch over his own. And his eye is good.

The psalm we read together just recapitulates what Hosea said, recounts the way God gathered his languishing people and gave them a safe dwelling place. "Give thanks to the Lord, for he is good, and his mercy endures forever . . . Ponder these things and consider well the mercies of the Lord."

Then lovely Colossians, a document of pure triumph, although here we find some reminders of our need to behave like God's people. The writer reminds us that we have been raised with Christ. All right then, act like it. We are to set our minds on "things above," not on "things below." That's figurative language of course, but he clears it up: if we died in Christ, then our life is now hidden in his resurrected life. We are being clothed in Christ by behaving like Christ, so when God's glory is fully revealed, we will be found in Christ. That being the case we have to modify our behavior, putting away "fornication, impurity, passion, evil desire, and greed." There's that list again, though if Paul really wrote this letter, I suspect the list would have been longer! And not only those carnal sins, but also sins of the soul: "anger, wrath, malice, slander, abusive language." And how we do talk about each other! Elsewhere Paul reminds us that our tongues are flamethrowers with which we scorch our brethren instead of loving them. Someone said that words are the skin of raw thoughts, so we must set a guard on the way we speak. And when we try to live that way, fail though we shall, God loves us for the try, "renews us in knowledge according to God's own image . . . so that Christ becomes all in all." A hymn of sweet victory as we are all assumed into God's boundless goodness.

Then the gospel, and as usual there's real meat on the bone here. You heard the story. A man in a crowd asks Jesus to make his brother split "the family inheritance" with him. Oh my. How people do fight over inheritance. I read somewhere that research reveals than an astonishing percentage of the litigation in American courts has to do with inheritance. Just recently, the family of some fabulously rich dowager in New York went through a super ugly court fight over her billions, as if a billion or two wouldn't be enough. And it starts early. When my girls were little, they'd stand in front of the china cabinet, all the wedding gifts on display, and Ginna would say, "That is going to be mine," and Carrie would say, "Well, that's going to be mine." And poor Stephen would wonder, "What's gonna be mine?" I told him all the Waterford is mine, so he can have that. Oh, we start it early. Just think: a person is gone from this world, a life and many loves whisked away—and those who should grieve instead fall to fighting over things. Greed, one of the seven deadly sins. Jesus warned us that the love of money, which is an extrapolation of things, is at the root of all evil. Not money, but the love of money. Well, Jesus rebukes the fellow and tells a story. A rich man, already had oodles, everything he needed, more, is blessed by a rich harvest, so much his barns won't hold it. What will he do? You notice, he doesn't consider contributing it to a food bank. Oh, no. He'll build more barns. At home in the U.S. I am amused by the thriving public storage business. All over the place, in high dollar neighborhoods and not so high dollar places, you'll find vast warehouses, some of them air-conditioned, thank you, to hold people's stuff. They've got so much stuff they can't fit it all into their houses. Do they stop buying up more stuff? No, they take it to those barns. Well, then this rich fellow considers how much fun that will be. "I will say to my soul"—at least he knows he's got one—"Soul, you've got it laid in the shade, eat, drink, and make merry." Oh, how smug. Building barns to hoard up his wealth and speculate on it, that he sees as an act of the soul. I admit, it's good business, but an action in the soul? Then circumstance imposes. This. Very. Night. I'm telling you, we all need to remember that. We're all young and healthy and beautiful here, God knows, but the rude fact is, we may not make it home all in one piece today. Could happen. Does happen. All at once, we vanish—and what will happen to all our stuff then? What good is it to us then? I've told you the story about the rich fellow who dies in a little town, and the whole place is abuzz with how much he left and to whom. If you've lived in a little town, you know how that goes. And one sage fellow, asked how much Mr. Gotrocks left, muses, "You know, I do believe he left it all." The folly of reducing a soul created for glory to nothing more significant than a checkbook. Rich in things and poor in soul, as the old hymn puts it.

Now this parable is not a condemnation of wealth. You may have heard it read that way; I sure have. But I don't believe it. There's nothing inherently wrong with wealth. God is the God of the rich as well as the poor, and therein lies part of his great justice. This parable condemns locating our own personal worth in the things we collect, the way we strive not to be better but rather to have more. The consumer culture we live in feeds on that urge. We are bombarded day by day with advertisements nagging us to spend money we don't have on things we don't need; and if we resist, well by golly there's something wrong with us! Remember the cabbage patch dolls years ago? Parents throttled each other in stores to get the horrible little things; otherwise they weren't good parents. Today I laugh when I hear the commercials for Sewell Cadillac in Dallas, all about "the automobile buying experience." Breathy voiced testimony, "They were compassionate and understanding, so flexible, they let us be ourselves, made us so welcome." I'll just bet. And today on television I heard someone assure that "this is the car buying experience as it should be." Give me a break. As if acquiring a vehicle is a great movement in the soul, tantamount to religious conversion, an apotheosis. What a lot of hooey. How we lap it up. Jesus warns us here: we have more to do in this life than latch onto stuff; we have an immortal soul to save and a God to glorify. Life is not measured in goods. Life is measured in God's goodness and our enormous luck to be part of it.

All right, if we are to lay up treasures in heaven, what are heavenly treasures? We know what earthly treasures are, and so long as we don't substitute them for God, I'm all for 'em. But what are those heavenly treasures we are to lay up, to cherish, to measure ourselves by? Well, I think at least three are those we've already considered today. It's a treasure that we are cleansed by God. When we consider what a bunch of unprofitable servants we often are, it's a treasure to know that God loves us in spite of everything and reassures us of forgiveness any time we ask for it. That's a treasure. It's another that God protects us, that he offers us a chance to get it right, to modify our behavior so that our lives in Christ and in the Holy Spirit fit us for the Kingdom of Heaven. That's a treasure. Another is just the knowledge that God is good, not angry and wrathful—I've heard the wrath of God defined as the love of God as it is experienced by those who reject it—that God always comes to us in goodness to govern us and rule us and set our feet on the upward way. That's a treasure.

I am so thankful for the chance this morning to proclaim the goodness of God and to revel in it with you. Life often seems to withhold God's goodness from us. Wicked people often seem to have all the fun, all the luck, and all the stuff. Good people often seem to go in want and hunger and pain and sadness and suffering of all kinds. Little children are born with lethal diseases. At times it's not easy to see God's goodness. Today's lessons, thank God for them, are a blessed reminder and a sorely needed reassurance of the most important fact we can know about our own lives and the lives of all God's family, our own family in the church but also all the rest of God's creation. And that important fact is simple. God. Is. Good.

Amen.

7 August 2016

Twelfth Sunday after Pentecost

Isaiah 1:1, 10-20 Psalm 50:1-8, 22-23 Hebrews 11:1-3, 8-16 Luke 12:32-40

If you've been coming to church regularly the past few weeks you may have noticed how the collects in the long Pentecost season seem at times to assume an almost childlike simplicity in form and theme. Today's is like that, at first glance anyway. We ask God to give us the spirit to think and do what is right so we can live according to his will. How simple and how complete. After all, when we finally realize that God loves us and wants to share our lives, the main thing we want to know is, "What do you want us to do?" How should we act out our lives as God's children? So so simple. Yet there are a couple of key words in there that need some defining, namely right and will. What in fact is right? And what exactly is God's will? Well folks, those are questions that have been pondered before, matters about which wars have been fought, so I think when we say Amen to that prayer we should have some notion what it is we're asking for. As I began to think about what the Holy Spirit wants the church to hear this morning, that preoccupied me; and sure enough I found considerable help in today's lessons. Let's have a look.

This morning we continue our visits with the Old Testament prophets, and today we meet Isaiah, the alpha prophet—the longest prophetic book and the most read and quoted of them all. Actually scholars think there were three prophets involved in creating the book that came down to us, but we won't go into that. Aren't ya glad? No, I think it's enough to say that the lesson today comes from the early Isaiah, a young man who lived when the Land of Judah was in tall cotton, sitting pretty, fat and happy, rich and satisfied. They thought. But as we've noted before, prophets are people who look way beyond the surface of circumstances, into the dark hearts of unloving people in power, rulers, and point out how they trample people in their way and in their grip. And he doesn't pull his punches, calls them "rulers of Sodom . . . and Gomorrah!" And that's for openers. Then, of all things, he lights into them for their worship. The temple was going full force, people coming in, changing money (from which the temple took a cut) to buy livestock—anywhere from a couple of sickly pigeons to feedlot-fat oxen—to be chopped up and burnt on the altars, the good meat handed on to the priests and Levites and their families, the dross thrown down the hillside into Gehenna. I mean, going to church was going to a slaughterhouse, a *rastro*, lots of blood and goo. But that's what they thought they should be doing, what the temple management required of them, so they did it on steroids. Isaiah says all that's repugnant to God, all the rams and fat beasts, rivers of blood. Of course to cover up the stink they used incense: "Incense is an abomination to me!" (Boy, in the old days when the High Church-Low Church wars were on, any priest who got out a thurible and started making smoke got that thrown at him!) All of the falderal, all the church kalendar and the sabbath rules and the solemn assemblies are hateful because they come: With. Iniquity. That's the rub. God can put up with our weird cults easily enough, but not when the hearts that offer them are wicked, when the hands that lift them up smoke with blood. So what does God want?

Comes next. "Cease to do evil, learn to do good; seek justice, rescue the oppressed, defend the orphan, plead for the widow." Oh. That. Well yes, that. Nothing fancy. Don't have to spend any money to get it. Don't need to cover it up with incense. Just those old-fashioned thirty-nine cent dime store variety virtues everybody knows are right. Fairness, compassion, generosity, sharing, protecting. Not complicated, childlike in fact. Like the fellow who said he couldn't define pornography but he knew it when he saw it. That, says Isaiah, is what is right, that word we're trying to define in the collect. It's not all the praying and taking on we do that pleases God, accords with God's will, but rather the self-evidently right things we do. Though our sinfulness be like scarlet cloth—one of my favorite old gospel hymns, Though your sins be as scarlet / They shall be as white a snow!—that kind of behavior, right behavior, earns forgiveness and God's reward, "the good of the land." See? There we've got help knowing what's doing right and living according to God's will.

The psalm is a recap of that whole passage. God sees plenty of sacrifices, "always before me," but what he wants is gratitude—and for his people to "keep my way." From Isaiah we've just learned a good bit about that way, God's will. It's love and kindness and compassion, all that. Well, all right, we can buy that; but what about . . . circumstances? A lot of the time, try as we might, all that doesn't seem to get us very far down the line, a lot of the time the bad guys get all the goodies and the good guys (that's us, of course) get shoved in a ditch. Trying to do right doesn't seem to pay off very well, and it's not surprising that people get discouraged and sometimes decide to throw in the towel and go with the flow. For help with that, let's turn to the epistle.

Hebrews is a complex book. Though it's attributed to Paul, most scholars agree he didn't write it. In the first place, the Greek is too good. Paul's Greek was pretty good but not artful. This letter was written by an artist, lots of elegant phrasing, rhetorical figures, elaborate logic that all goes in a straight line, not much like what we find in the rest of Paul. But we won't worry about that. We know who the audience was: the Christians in Jerusalem who were having a hard time. They were under persecution, the Jewish community was on them hard to forget all that Jesus stuff about goodness and so on and get back in line and pay their temple taxes like everybody else. The writer spends a lot of time trying to call them back to their Christian commitment, and to do that he rehearses their whole history. Today we pick him up well into the book, and the key word in the reading is faith, shows up eight times in three paragraphs. And thanks, Sandy, for emphasizing it every time you read it this morning, because it needs to be right in our faces. As you've heard from me before, faith is not saying you believe something you don't, a kind of contradiction in terms; my favorite definition is that faith is a corroborated notion, something you can't prove but you just have a hunch and you see evidence all around. The writer today says it is "assurance of things hoped for, the conviction of things not seen." Then he rehearses the way Abraham, the great ancestor of Israel, dealt with a perfectly preposterous proposition. You know the story. He was seventy, nearly as old as a lot of us, so was his wife. He was rich as rich could get then, but he had no children, no heir to carry on his line and preserve his wealth—remember last Sunday's gospel, all that about inheritance? And then one night three men show up out of the blue, angels we learn later, and tell him to pack it all up and go to another place. Now how much sense does that make? None. Later they'll also promise him he and Sarah are going to have a son. She overhears that and has a laugh. Later they promise him his progeny will be like the sands of the sea. Now not one word of that makes any sense, none at all. But know what? At his stage of life, it looked every bit as good as the alternative. So he decided to take the bait, made a bet, and set out for the promised land. That took faith in industrial loads. But ask yourself: how many times have you heard someone propose something absolutely outrageous, something against all the odds, and yet . . . you look down the line, you consider who's offering, you figure it's at least as plausible as the alternatives, and you make a decision. "Think I'll take you up on that." Sometimes it's folly, but other times it's glory. Pascal, the seventeenth century French philosopher, was an agnostic at best, but he followed the church's rules, even wore a hair shirt. He figured that God was as plausible as not-God, so he'd just hedge that bet. Basically that's an existentialist position: it's not what you can prove, not what you believe, but what you commit to, what you do that counts. You see, faith is a two way street: Abraham believed that the one who promised him was faithful, would deliver, and even though the odds were all against it, he decided to throw in with the one he trusted, so he got moving. That's the way faith energizes us: we trust God's promise of rewarding our good performance, so we perform, even though we often don't seem to be getting much reward. The writer notes that from Abraham forward, the Israelites had been swimming upstream and seemingly losing the fight. Yet they saw a light, glimpsed it from afar and followed it, which God found pleasing and prepared a dwelling place for them. The same is true for God's children, for the church, us today. We trust the God who calls us, so even when the going is not good, we put our heads into the wind and march. Do what is right to live in accordance with God's will and let the reward come when God's ready to give it—and he always does. Faith and faithfulness.

On to the gospel. Luke continues last Sunday's hymn of love and reassurance, assures the flock of the Father's love and the promise of the Kingdom, tells them to quit worrying, give alms to the poor and lay treasures for themselves in Heaven, more from last week. Then he tells a little parable about how they must think of themselves as servants and stay ready for their master's return from a feast, get things ready to make him welcome and take care of his every need or whim. If they do all that—we might equate that with doing the right thing in the collect—they're in for a great surprise, because when the master gets there, instead of waiting for them to wait on him, he'll throw off his greatcoat, put on a footman's livery, and invite them all to the table where he will serve them! Why would he do such a thing? Because they have been behaving according to his will, being kind and generous and compassionate, being clothed in him as we've read in Colossians, doing all those little daily acts of kindness that hold the world together. "Look at you! You've all got on your wedding garments!" And he invites them to the banquet. But there's a little caveat at the end: don't ever think your work is done, don't get to feeling smug and satisfied, because the battle is not yet won, not by any means, and the master—the Son of Man—is coming when you least expect it. That line is often taken as apocalyptic, a kind of "Repent! The End is near!" warning, and I reckon it is in a way, though I don't find it very useful to me. Rather I like to take that as a reminder that Jesus comes to check on me all the time, that I'm going to run into somebody this very day who needs a kind word, a helping hand, a healing touch, a listening ear, and that if I miss that encounter I've let the thief make off with my reward. In any case, the whole passage is comforting. Some decades ago when I was rector in McKinney, Texas, the little parish in Bonham over to the east went vacant and the bishop asked me to supply there for a while, couple, three months. I drove up and we said prayers on Sunday afternoons. And oh they were scared, afraid the place was going to close, that they'd failed, that they had no future. I remember that the last Sunday I served them, this passage from Luke was the gospel lesson, and I could reassure them: "Fear not, little flock, it is your Father's good will to give you the Kingdom." So they kept the doors open and the lights lit and their arms open, and that congregation is doing very well to this good day.

You see? It's not complicated. It's simple. It's just not always easy. We know pretty well what the right thing to do is. How many of you saw *The Bonfire of the Vanities*, a great movie with Tom Hanks and some others? Came out some years back, all about a bunch of self-satisfied people living off other people's backs, just like the bunch in Isaiah this morning. In the end the whole mess ends up in a wonderful trial scene where Morgan Freeman played the judge who found them all absolutely disgusting. After he pronounces judgment, he lectures them and basically says, "For God's sake, go home and behave! Stop lying and cheating and fooling around and behave! Behave the way your grandmother taught you" Oh, I really like that because it gets us right back to that childlike simplicity. We know what we ought to do, so do it. God will take care of the reward, and the reward is not what we're in it for anyway. We're in it because God has called us to share the glory of redeeming the hurting world around us, so instead of pining for what is not, we hitch up our britches and get moving. We don't always see the reward, and sometimes doing the right thing can be right expensive. But we lend a helping hand to this one and take another step. We comfort that one and take another step. We seek justice and defend the orphan and plead for the widow and take another step. We do it because it's right and because we've seen that light from afar. We have accepted an outrageous proposition because we trust the proposer. And our trust, our faith in that glorious outrage gives us the gumption to go on trusting and doing. Childlike and simple. Fear not, little flock, for it is your Father's good pleasure to give you the Kingdom.

Amen.

Though this photo was taken at Restaurante Axitla in Tepoztlán, a place not to miss if you visit, the vegetation is typical of the whole mountain range upon which Cuernavaca is built. The soil is volcanic, the temperature mild, the rain daily during the season, and the results are spectacular. You throw a seed into the air, and it will root and blossom before it hits the ground. This dry land Texan marvels.

14 August 2016

Thirteenth Sunday after Pentecost

Isaiah 5:1-7   Psalm 80:1-2, 8-19   Hebrews 11:29-12:2   Luke 12:49-56

    As some of you are aware, I'll be going home to Texas this week and won't be back among you for quite some time, not before Easter next year, so today is the last chance I'll have in a long time to preach and share the scriptures with you, a kind of farewell. Well, let me tell you if I had any choice I sure wouldn't have picked today's scary lessons for the occasion! Wow! Did you ever? I mean the lessons have been so sweet and so reassuring and so enjoyable for most of the summer, such fun to explore—and then we come up with what you've just listened to. God in a bad humor all over the place! I remember once in my parish in Cleburne we had a baptism, sweet little baby to christen, but the lessons were all about the devil! Well, we drove the devil out of the baby, but today we don't even have a baby, just these scary lessons. No hint of that in the collect, which again is pure childlike simplicity. We thank God that he sent Jesus to be a sacrifice for sin and an example of holy life, then ask for grace to receive that gift and follow in Jesus' footsteps. Nice? Yes, wonderful. But then bing bang boom in the lessons.

    First that beautiful metaphor in Isaiah, the lover creating a vineyard for the belovèd, all that digging and delving and fencing and guarding. I've always thought God must be a farmer, because there are so many agricultural tropes in the Bible. I mean, the first thing God did with Adam, long before he created Eve, was to sit down and name all the critters he'd created, name all the livestock. And here the image is so gentle and loving—but it all turns out bad. The grapes turned out to be pure dee New York mustangs, sour as could be, and the planter is sorely disappointed. Why are the grapes sour? What did I not do for you? he asks. He is really let down. Often the Old Testament prophets aim their anger at the religious leaders and give the people of Israel a break. They're victims. But not here. God's own let him down, hard, and he is rueful. The psalm is just a hymn written on that exact theme, God's disappointment with his pleasant planting, though in the psalm at least the people see they've botched it. At the end the psalmist turns to God and asks for forgiveness: "Restore us, O Lord God of hosts; show us the light of your countenance and we shall be saved." But the failure is unavoidable. Then in Hebrews, the writer continues to tell of all the things the Israelites managed through faith, escaping the Red Sea, taking Jericho, conquering kingdoms and so on; but the story goes South, and we learn of people being tortured, chained, imprisoned, stoned to death, sawn in two, running around in animal skins, living in caves. The lesson ends with an affirmation. We are surrounded by a cloud of witnesses who have overcome adversity, so we must "lay aside every weight . . and run with perseverance the race that is set before us" as did Jesus. The point is, being God's chosen people has its reward, but the reward comes at a price. We don't just coast home; we have to carry our share of the load. Then the lesson from Luke. Mercy! The end of last week's gospel was, "It is the Father's good pleasure to give you the Kingdom," but today, "I came to bring fire to the earth, and how I wish it were already kindled!" That'll bring on a whiplash. Not peace but a sword, division in the household, two against three, parents against children, and everybody against the in-laws! Finally he calls them—calls us—hypocrites because we don't have the sense to see what's going on around us. Did you ever hear the like? That is the rough side of God's tongue, and Jesus absolutely lays it on.

Well now. As I considered how to grasp this nettle, my mind went straight into metaphysics, all about the theology of the atonement and Jesus' sacrificial death, how we participate in that, how baptism joins us in that suffering that produces joy . . . but then after a while I figured you don't deserve to sit through all that. I think it's all true and could drag you through it, but in the long run I'm not sure you'd feel very fed. Rather, like it's been so often this summer, I think we can get hold of this better if we stay pretty practical. There's a phenomenon I identified a long time back, something I call the Sweet Jesus Heresy, our preference for all the comforting things Jesus said, all his gentleness and kindness, to the exclusion of everything else. The notion that Jesus came to a really pretty nice world to make it even nicer. Once while I was in seminary we had a visiting priest from England as preacher who said that most American preaching could be reduced to one sentence: "I wish you would all try very hard to be very nice." Cheeky, I thought, but there's some truth in it. We like Jesus' message when it's easy, but when the tune changes, we tend to shy away. So let's try something simple. Ask yourself, "Is everything okay? Is everything in my life okay? I've got it made, don't I?" Well. Don't know about you, but I sure can't answer that with an unqualified Yes. If I'm honest I know there's a lot awry in my life, a lot of work left for me, some of it really painful. This morning for some reason I was recalling a bad memory, and I had to admit that if I had it all to do over again, I'd probably make the same mistakes again. I haven't learned a lot, and I'm surely not much stronger, just as prone to foolishness and wickedness as ever. And I imagine that most of us would have to make the same confession, not only about our personal lives but also about our lives together—as families, as a church, as a society. We make some headway, yes, but we fail just as often if not oftener. It hardly comes as a surprise. I mean, if everything were just ducky, then why Jesus in the first place? What did he come to save us from? As the poet said, we are betrayed by what is false within, and like it or lump it, we finally have to realize that following Jesus means taking a stand, making some sacrifices. Nobody got upset when Jesus talked about the birds of the air or the lilies of the field. But when he blasted greed and cruelty and hypocrisy, people got mad. When he quirted the moneychangers out of the temple, they tried to kill him. When he faced down the Roman empire and said his kingdom was mightier than all its power, when he denounced any system of belief or action that deforms and dismisses and destroys human life and dignity—they did kill him. And the amazing thing is, in all his condemnation of evil, he never fought fire with fire, never answered hate with hate but rather always with love and forgiveness and a call to repentance and a life grounded in love. He wept over Jerusalem as it reviled him, forgave the men who nailed him to the cross, promised the repentant thief a place in paradise, all this while he was in an agony we can hardly imagine. He gave up his peace to bring peace to our unpeaceful lives. That's what his baptism meant. He gave up his wholeness to take on our brokenness, to live as one of us, and to show us the way to reconcile our damaged and dying world with God's purpose, God's Kingdom. While I was thinking of all this metaphysically, it occurred to me that the whole Big Bang theory has a similar pattern. Creation was an explosion, smashing everything into countless tiny bits, and all our billions of years of history have been the story of that explosion expanding, then beginning to contract back upon itself, from chaos back into unity. Creation requires breakage. You gotta break eggs to make an omelet. Childbirth is a wondrous miracle, but it's right rough on the mother. God's creation—the universe we live in, us—came from breakage; Jesus came to show us how to live it back into wholeness, to holiness. It is glorious, but it comes at a price.

Well, let's come back to earth. No need to flog the horse any more. But how do we live that out? It's not complex. We, you and I, take up Jesus' cross and we oppose evil and cruelty and hatred and injustice and hypocrisy, not just in some kind of silent moral superiority but in word and deed, both. What's the saying here in Mexico? *Hechos, no palabras.* It's one thing to talk a big fight; it's another actually to step in and get our hands dirty cleaning up the world's messes. Opportunities come to us every day, and they don't need to be heroic. I am so proud of that groaning food basket at the door. You're finally getting into the habit of sharing from your abundance with people who go hungry day by day. That's a start, but it's by no means a Mission Accomplished moment, not by a long shot. As I am driven around in this gorgeous city, it's easy to cast my eyes upward and exult in the beauty of the skies, the mountain majesties on every horizon, the deliriously beautiful vegetation, flowers everywhere, all just intoxicating. But if you just lower that view a little you'll see five year old children hawking *chicle* and ancient women begging for coins, young people with nowhere to go juggling or swallowing fire or trying to wipe off your windshield. Peek through narrow doorways leading down into places where people live in abject squalor. The easy response is, Oh that's just too much to think about, I can't fix all that, I'm just one person. That's not what Mother Theresa said when somebody asked her how on earth she expected to take care of the thousands of homeless people in Calcutta. "One at a time," she said. That's what Jesus calls us to, to meet what life sends us day by day, to find something unloved and love it, not to shrink back in disgust or judgment but to gird up our loins and join the battle.

Now I know, I know. This congregation has been through a rough patch in the last year, and I'm aware of that; and a lot of us are as old as I am or older, and the whole enterprise is pretty stretched. Yet we're still here, the battle is all around us, and we have not yet been discharged from active service. A person who was important in my formation years ago was Bertrand Russell, the English philosopher and mathematician and atheist. When that man was eighty-nine years old, he got out into the streets of London and led a protest against Britain's participation in the nuclear arms race. There's a famous picture of him in a sit-down, looks like an enraged turkey! But old as he was, he was still in the fight. Each of us individually and surely all of us as a congregation need to stay in the fight as long as we have breath, because the battle is not yet won.

These lessons today call us to a reality check. They are an antidote to self-righteousness and self-satisfaction, something we're all prone to. They ask us, What has your Christianity cost you lately? If it doesn't hurt from time to time, that's a sign we need to exercise it more, harder. And like I said, it doesn't have to be heroic—although sometimes it is—but something as simple as a kind word to someone in distress, a cup of water, a bite to eat, a coin into a beggar's hand, a donation to charity, those little acts of generosity and goodness which are, as the collect says, the way we follow Jesus' footsteps.

Now to sweeten all this up, I want to do something a little out of the ordinary. There's a hymn we won't be singing today I want to read to you, because it says all I've tied to say so beautifully and sweetly and perfectly. I won't tell you which one it is so you won't grab a hymnal but just listen.

Come, labor on. Who dares stand idle on the harvest plain,
while all around us waves the golden grain?
And to each servant does the Master say, "Go work today."

Come, labor on. The enemy is watching night and day,
to sow the tares, to snatch the seed away;
while we in sleep our duty have forgot, he slumberèd not.

Come, labor on. Away with gloomy doubts and faithless fear!
No arm so weak but may do service here.
By feeblest agents may our God fulfill his righteous will.

Come, labor on. Claim the high calling angels cannot share—
to young and old the gospel gladness bear.
Redeem the time; its hours too swiftly fly. The night draws nigh.

Come, labor on. No time for rest till glows the western sky,
till the long shadows o'er our pathway lie,
and a glad sound comes with the setting sun—"Servants, well done."

Amen.